This book belongs to.....

....

....

Small preview of what's inside

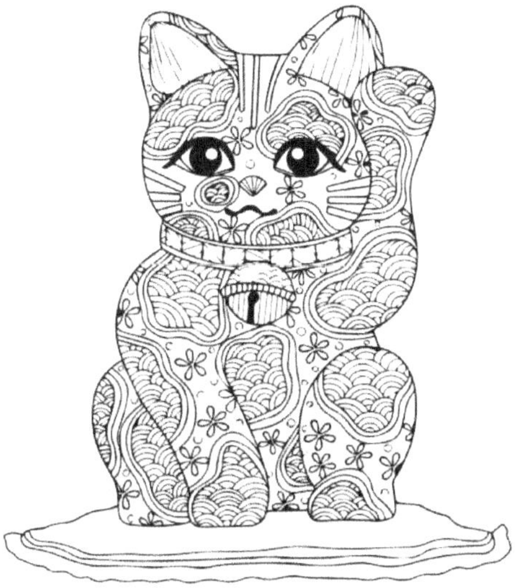
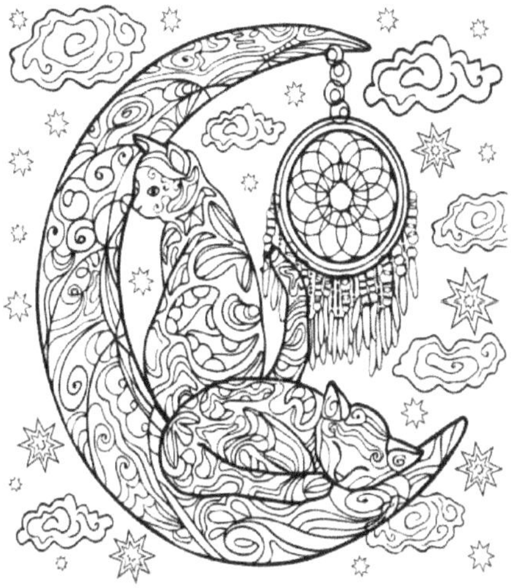
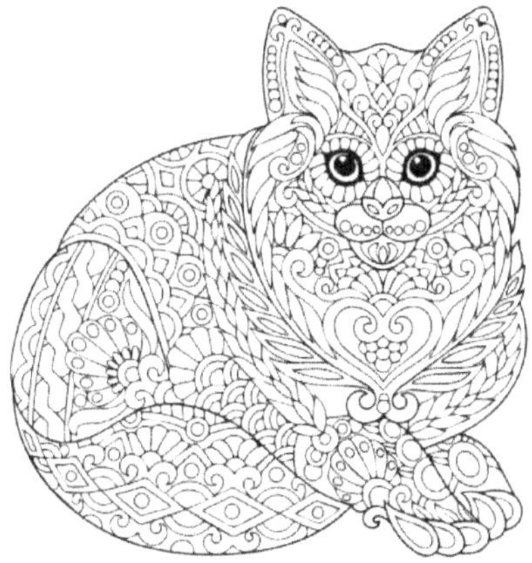
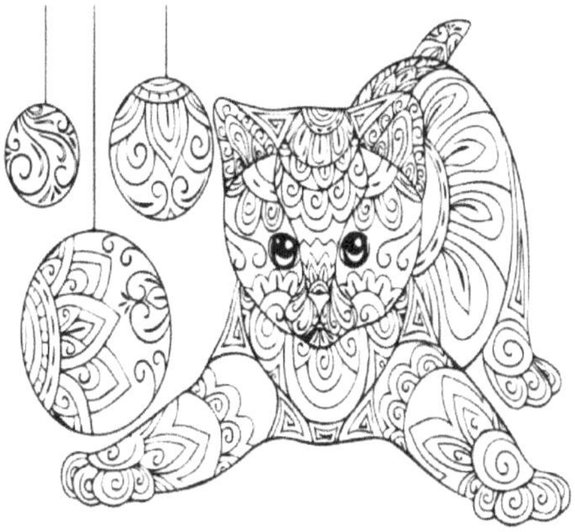
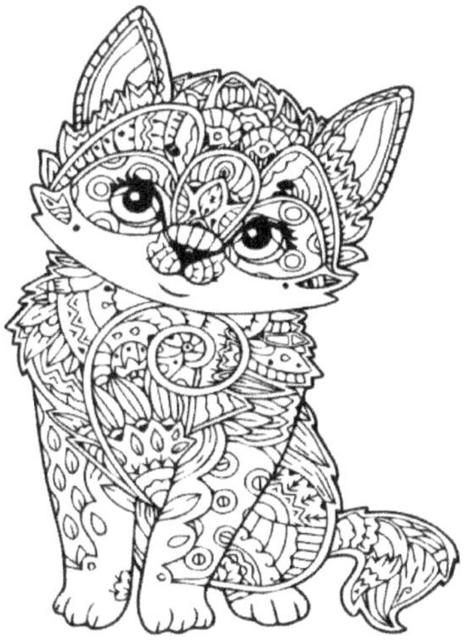
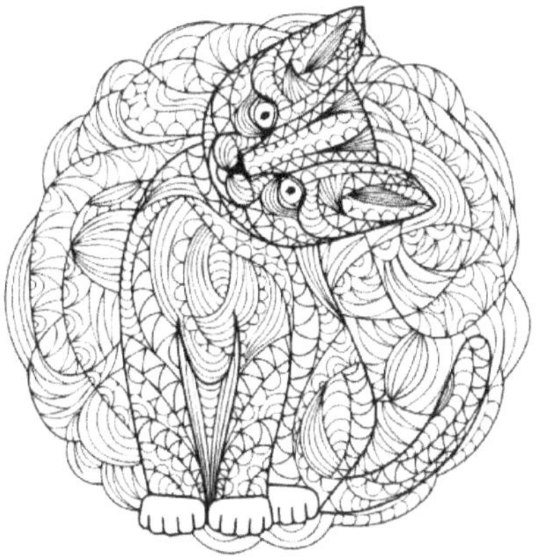

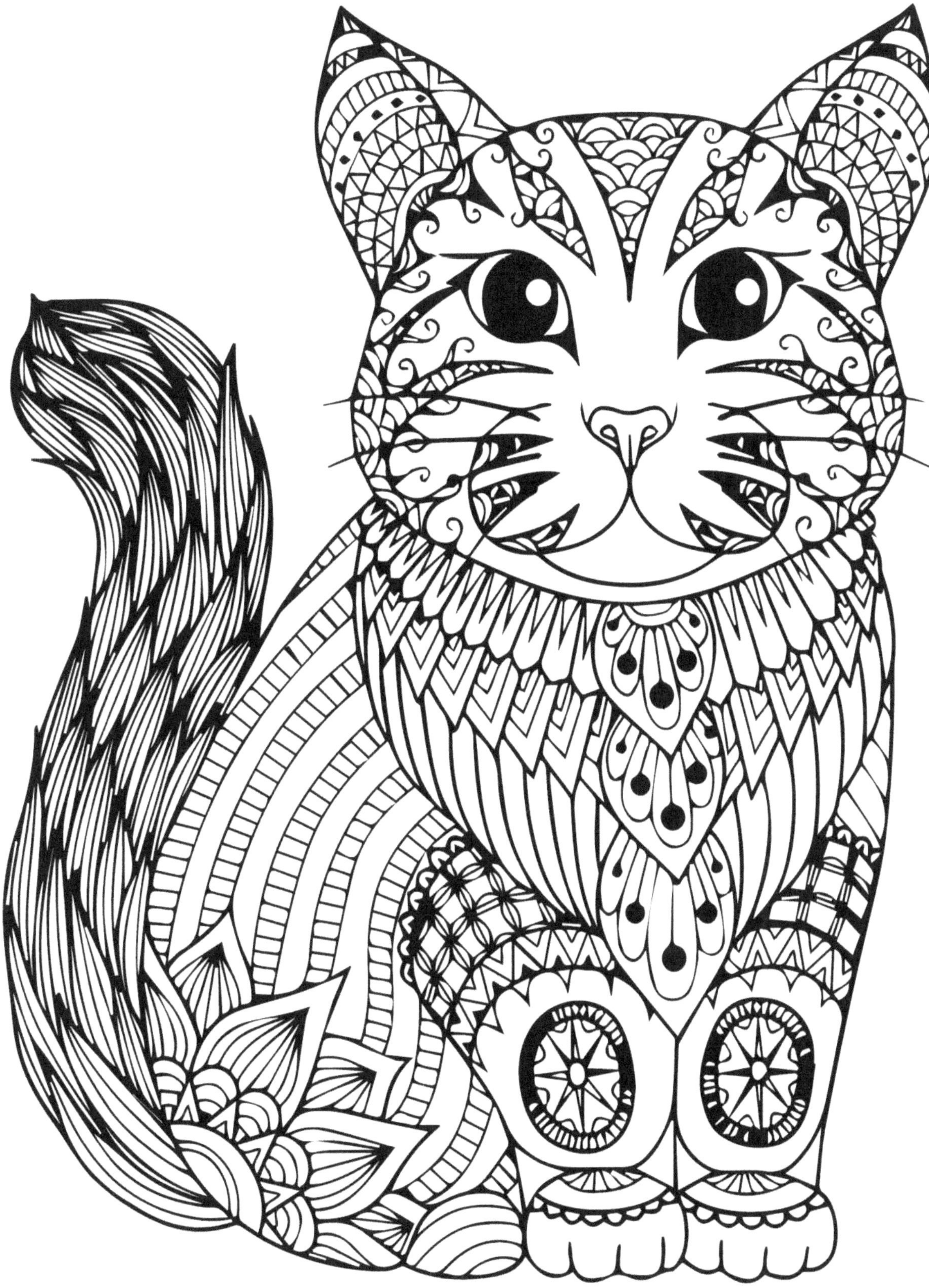

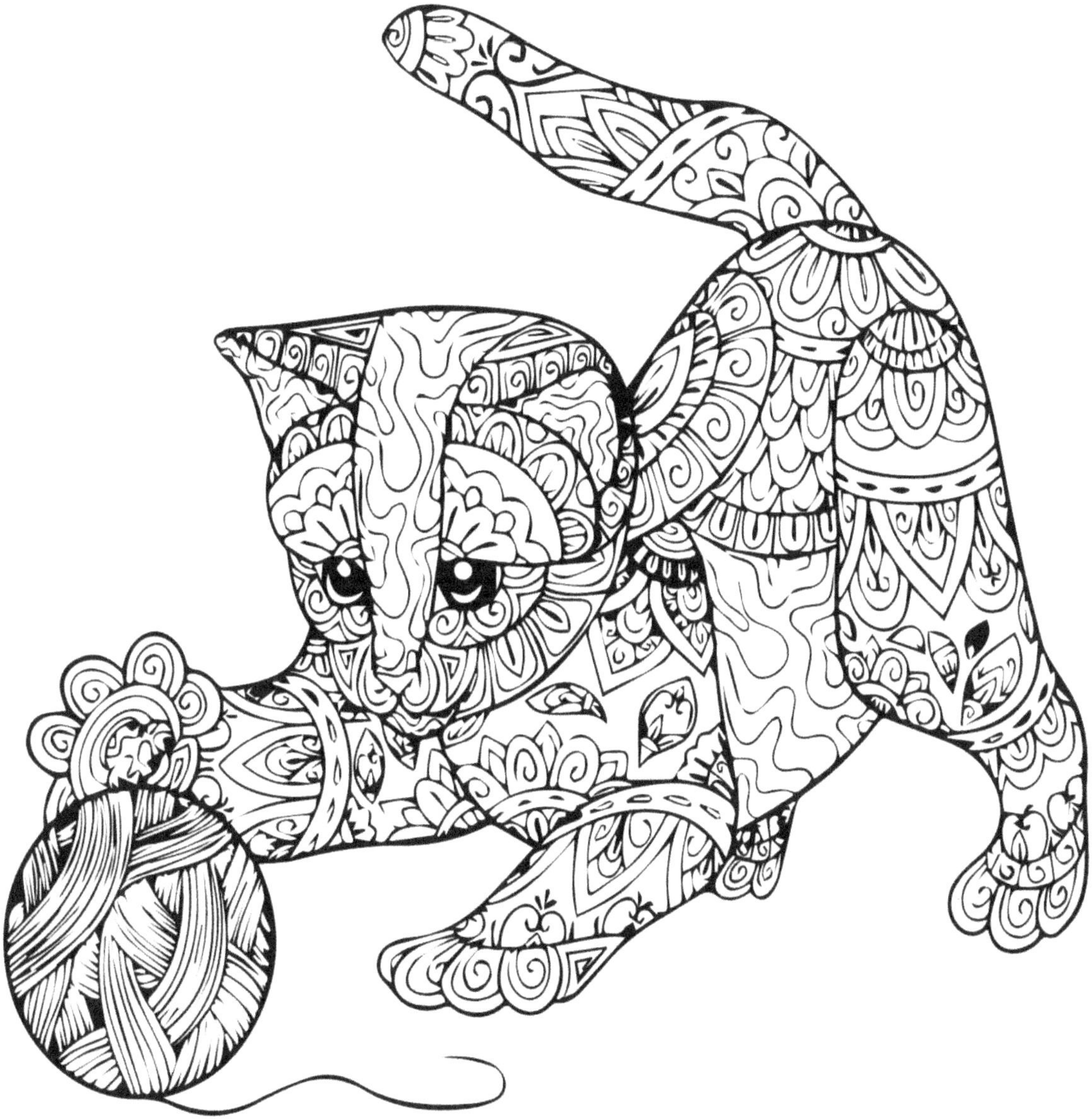

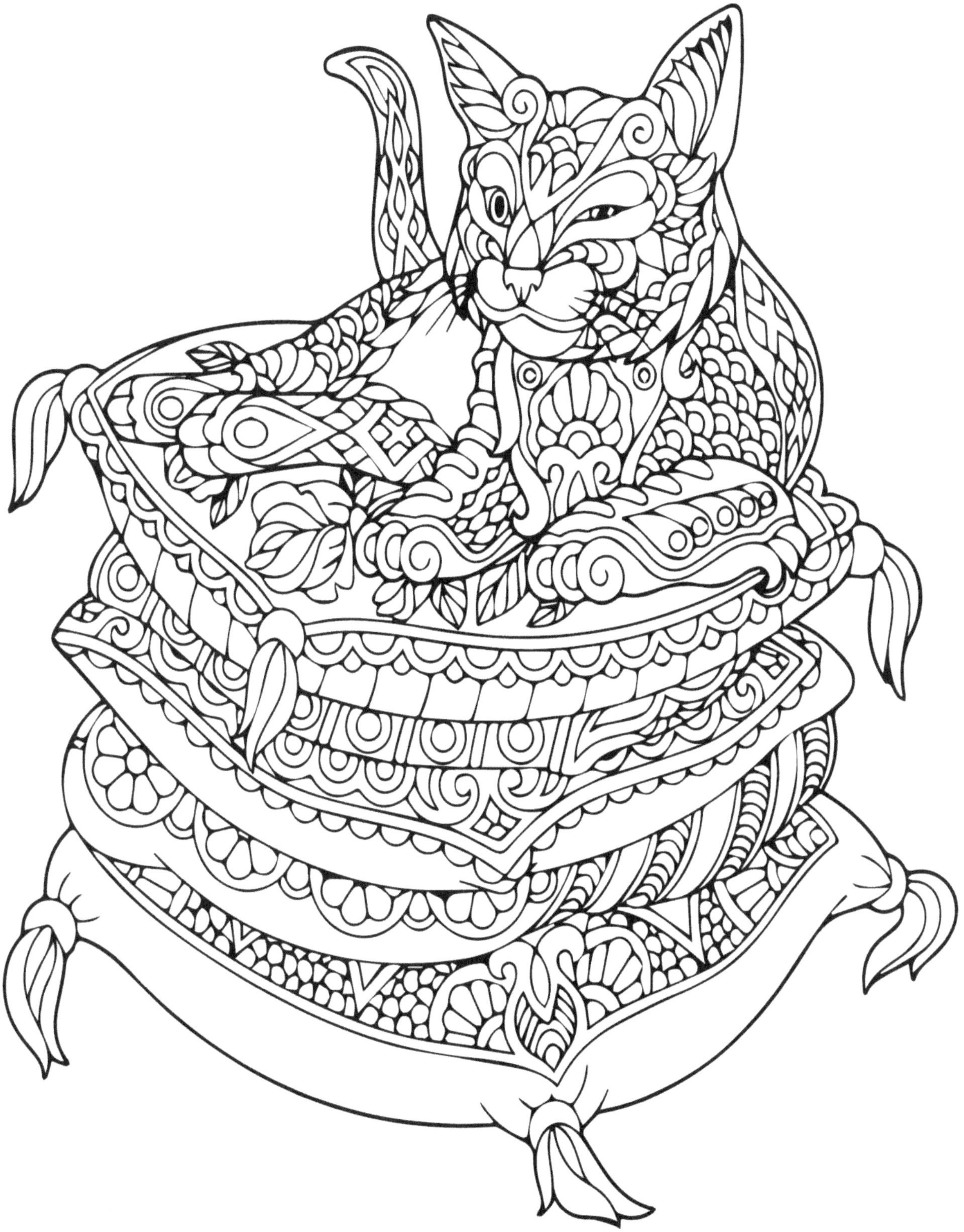

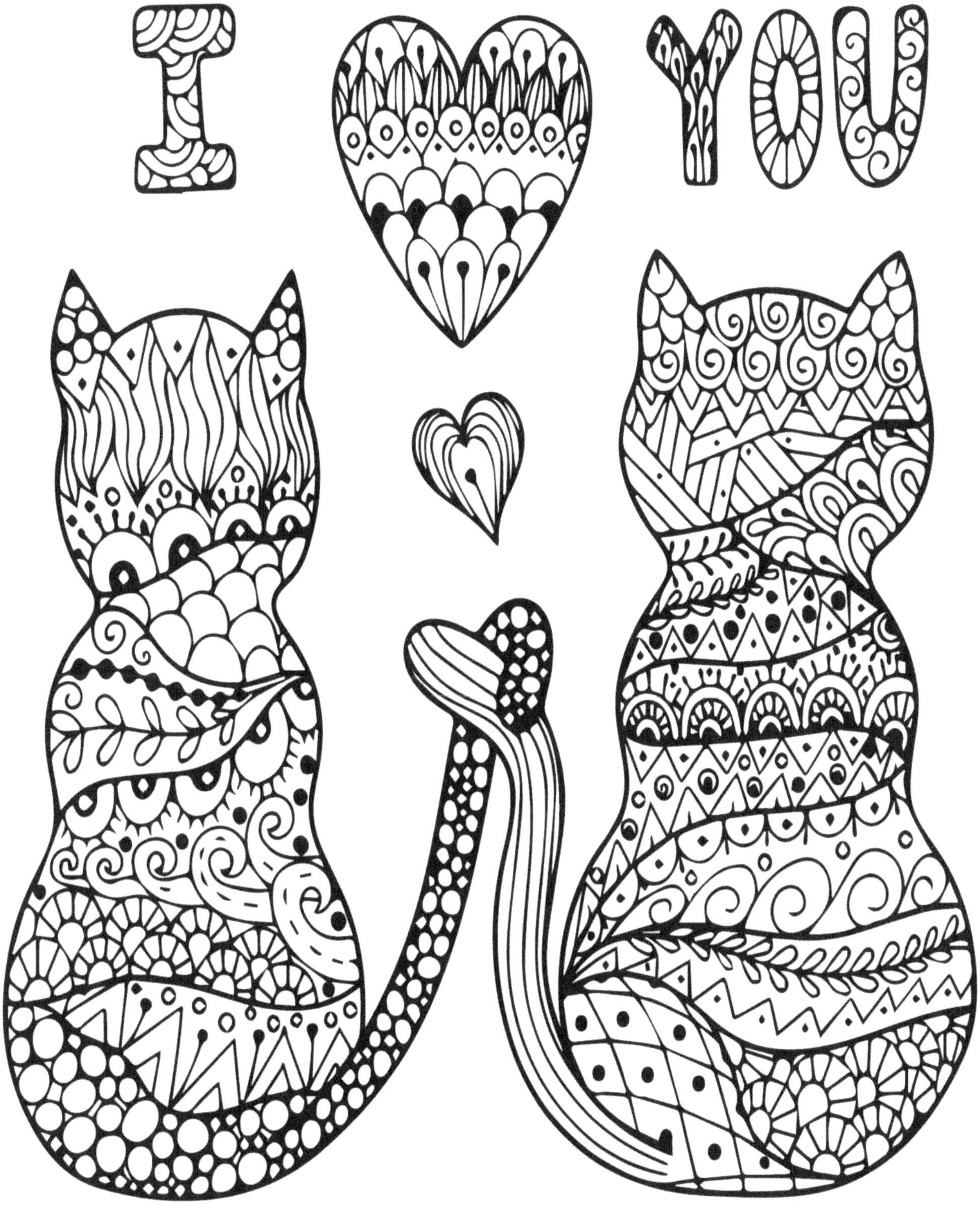
I
YOU

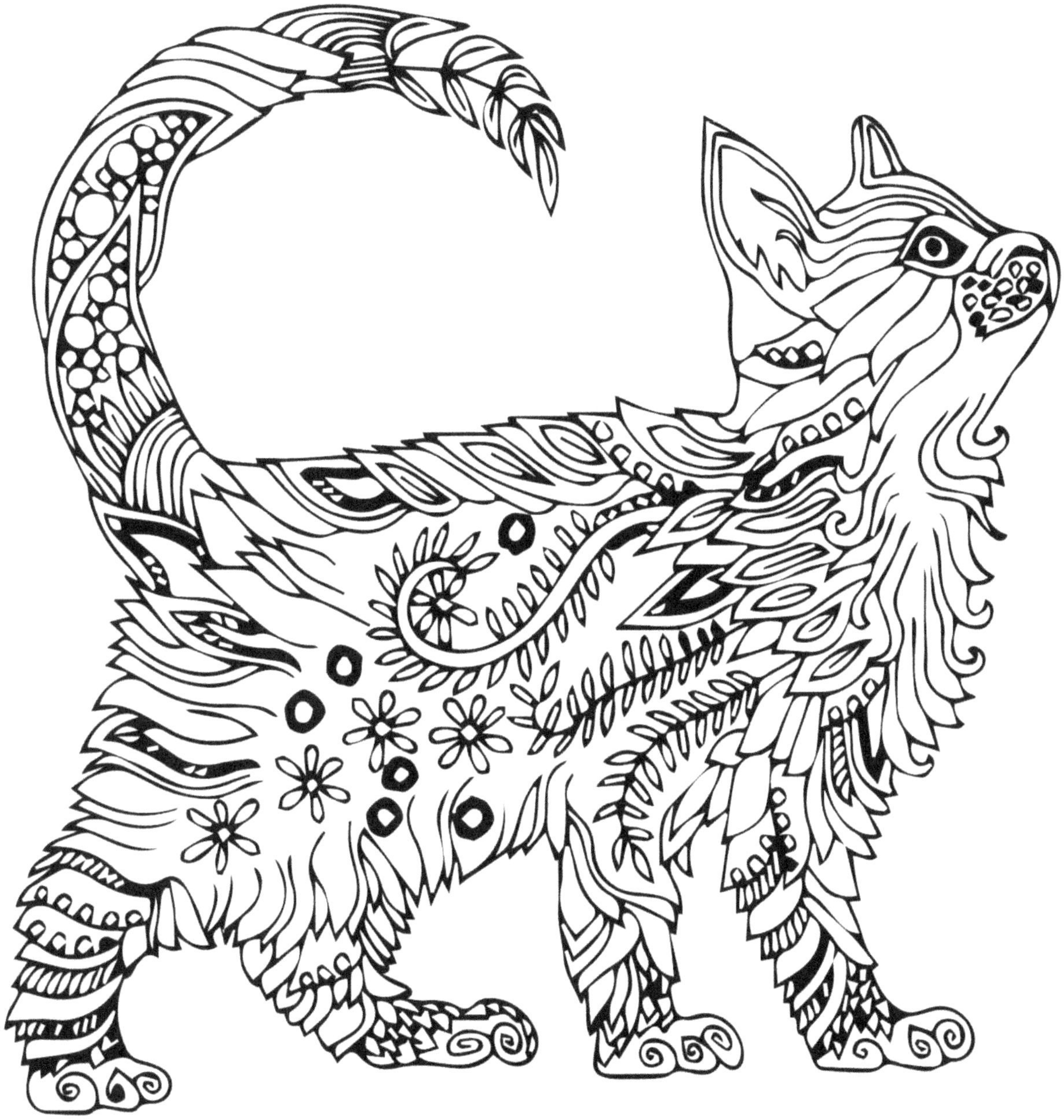

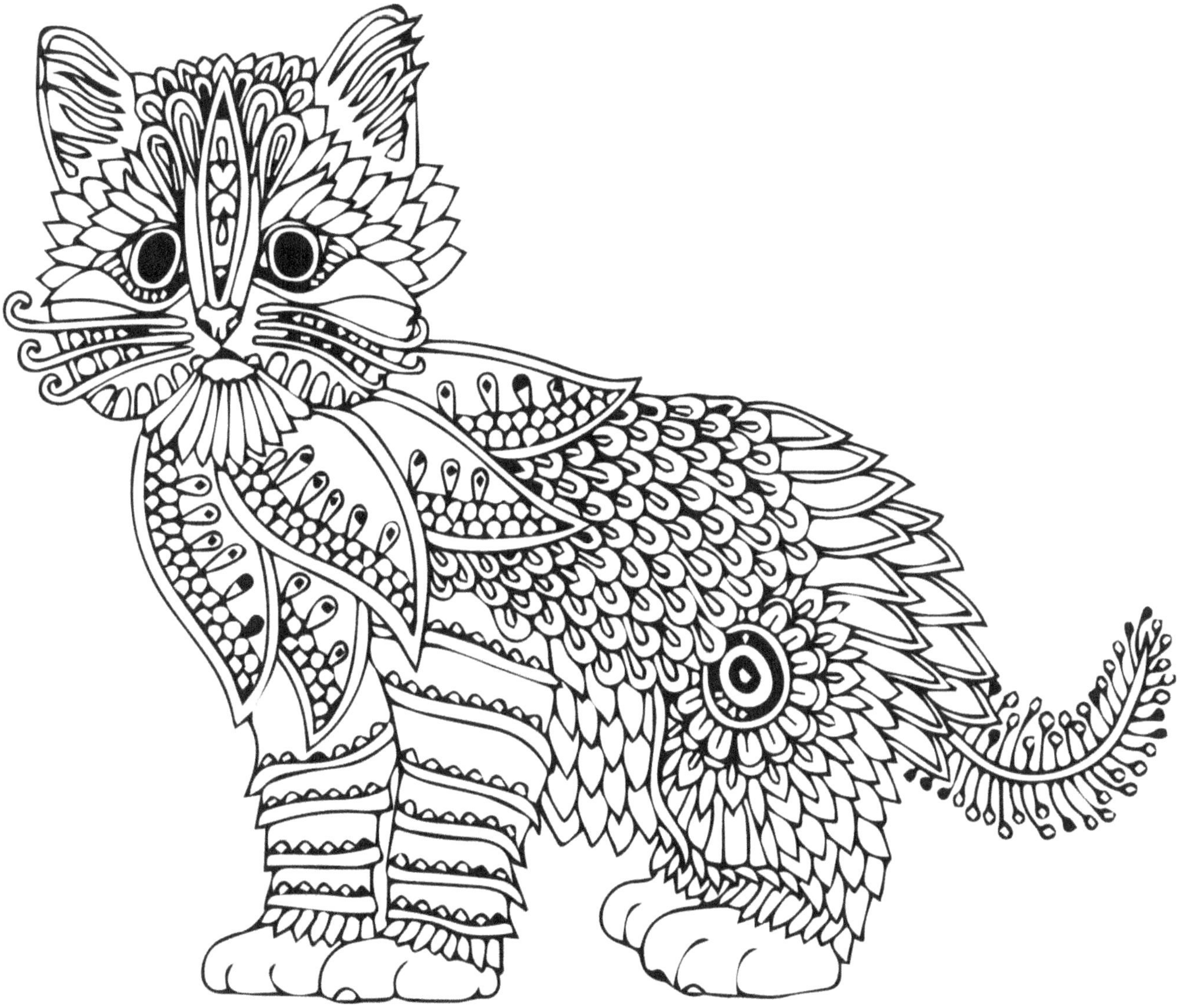

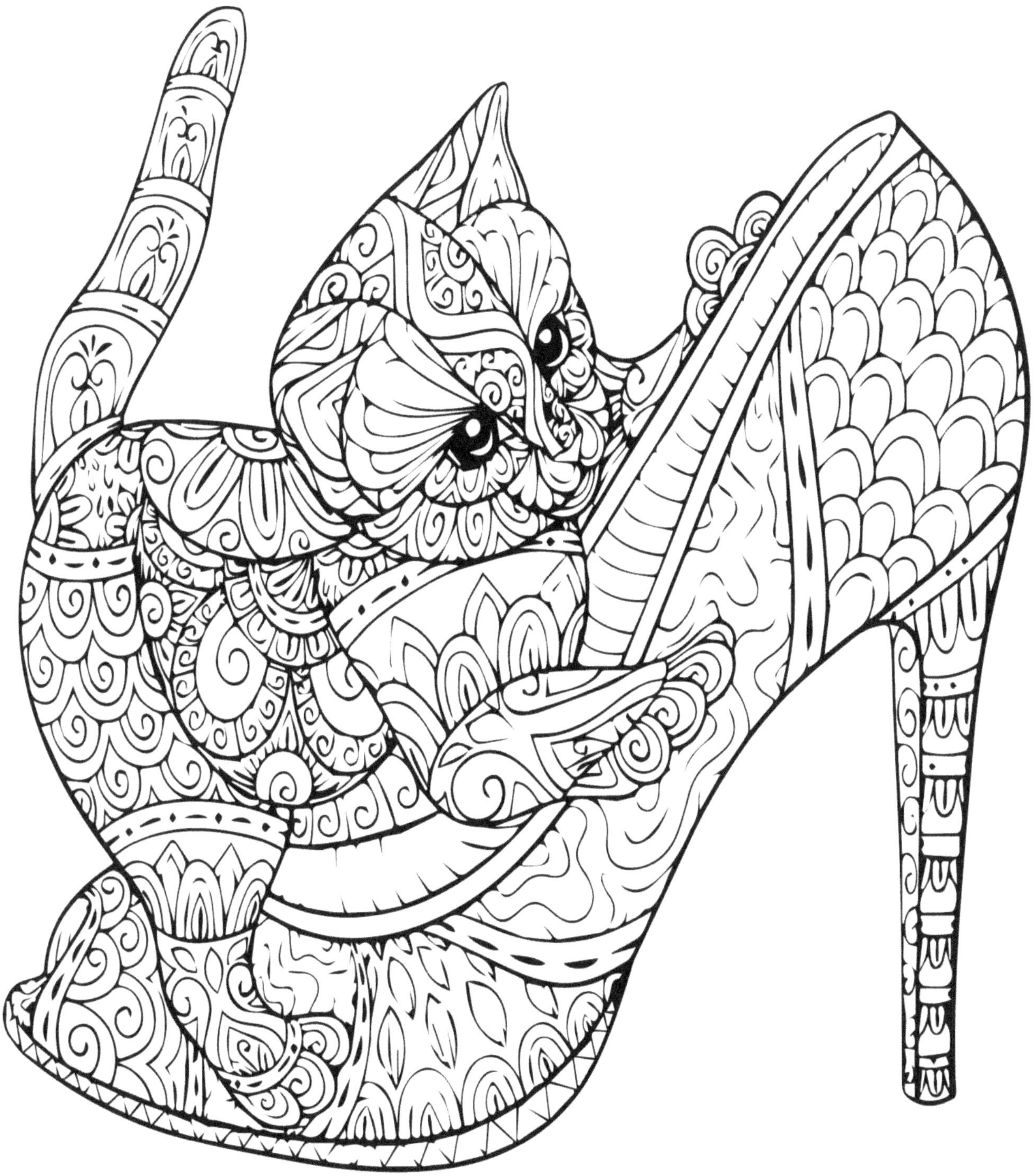

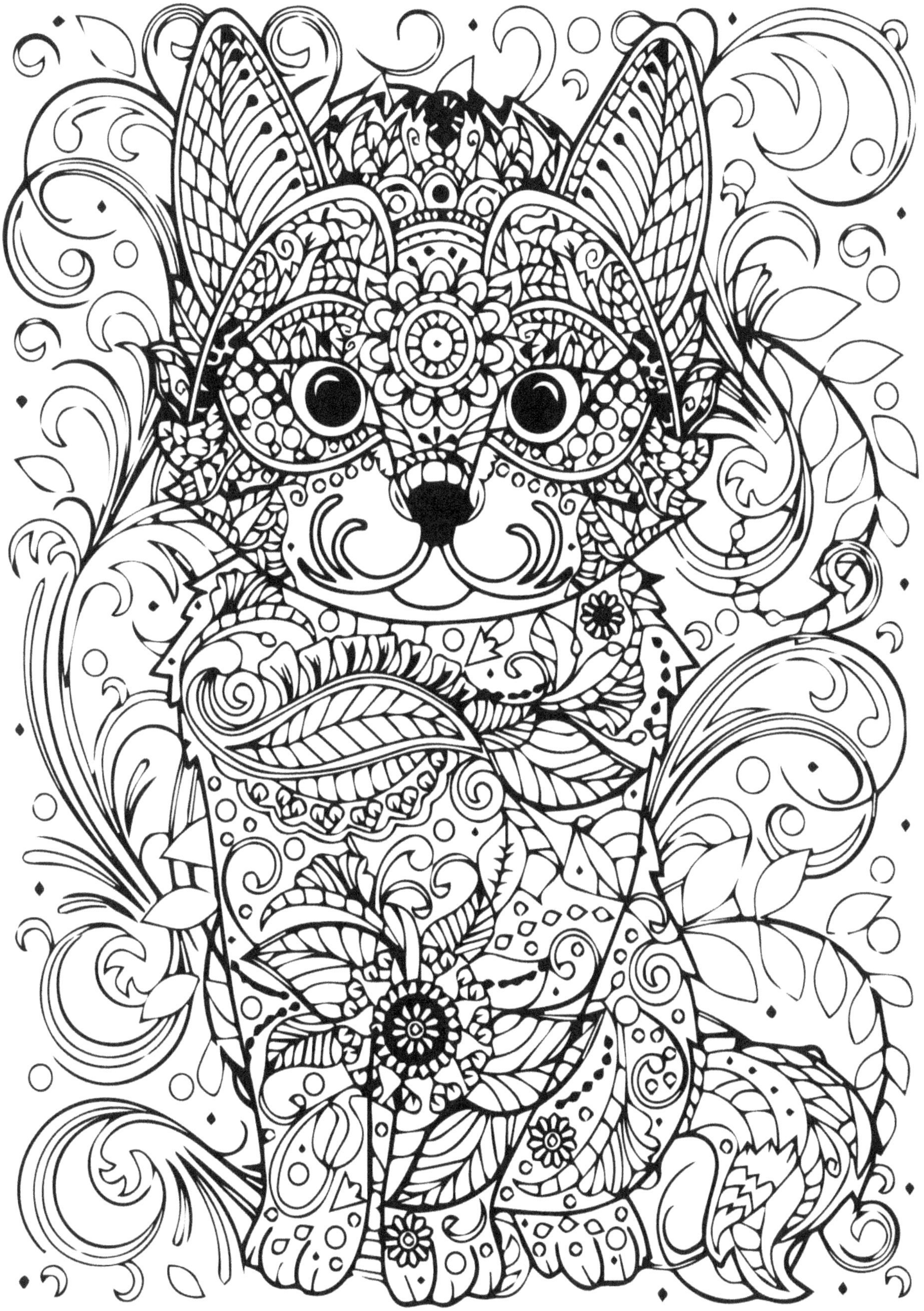

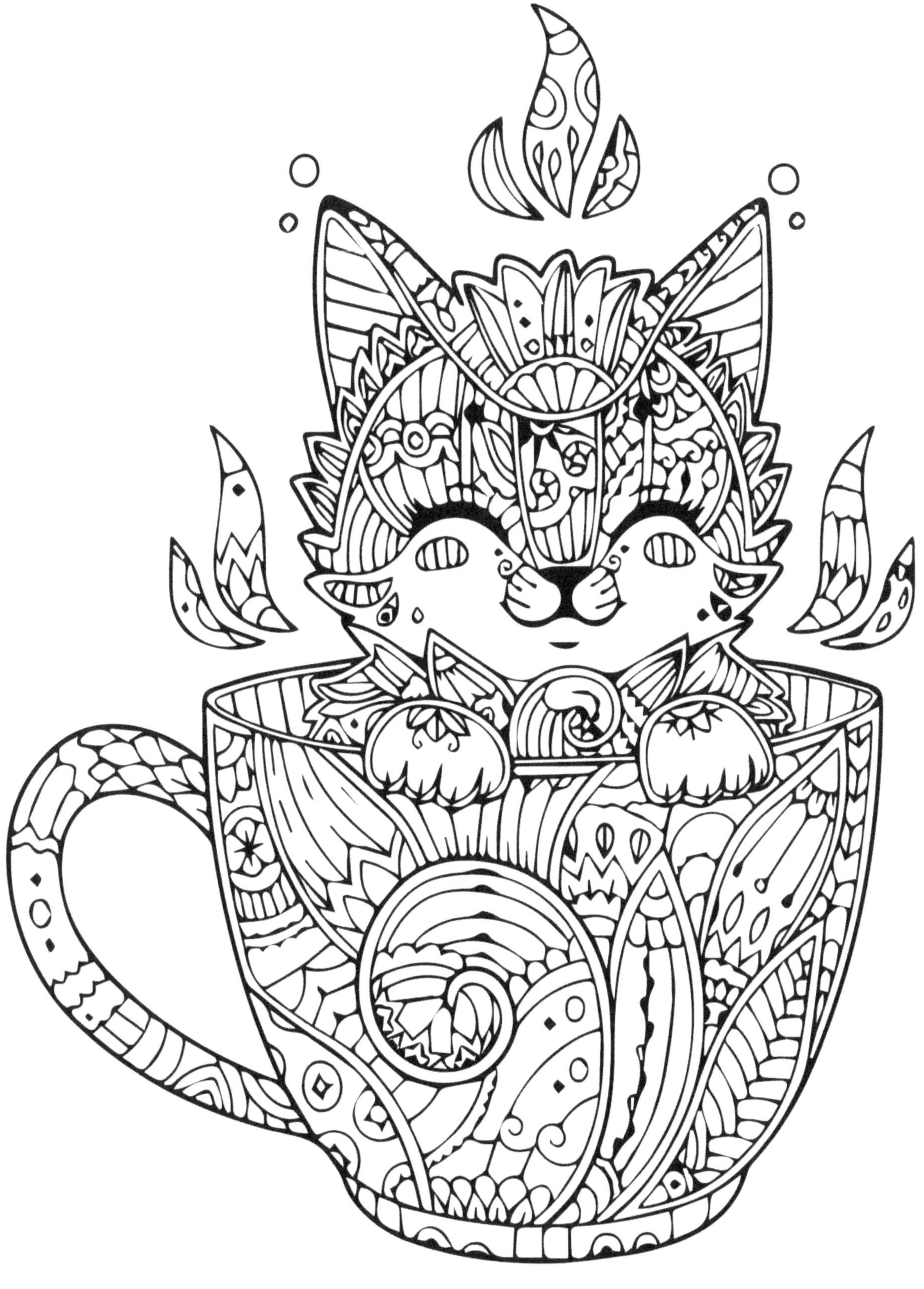

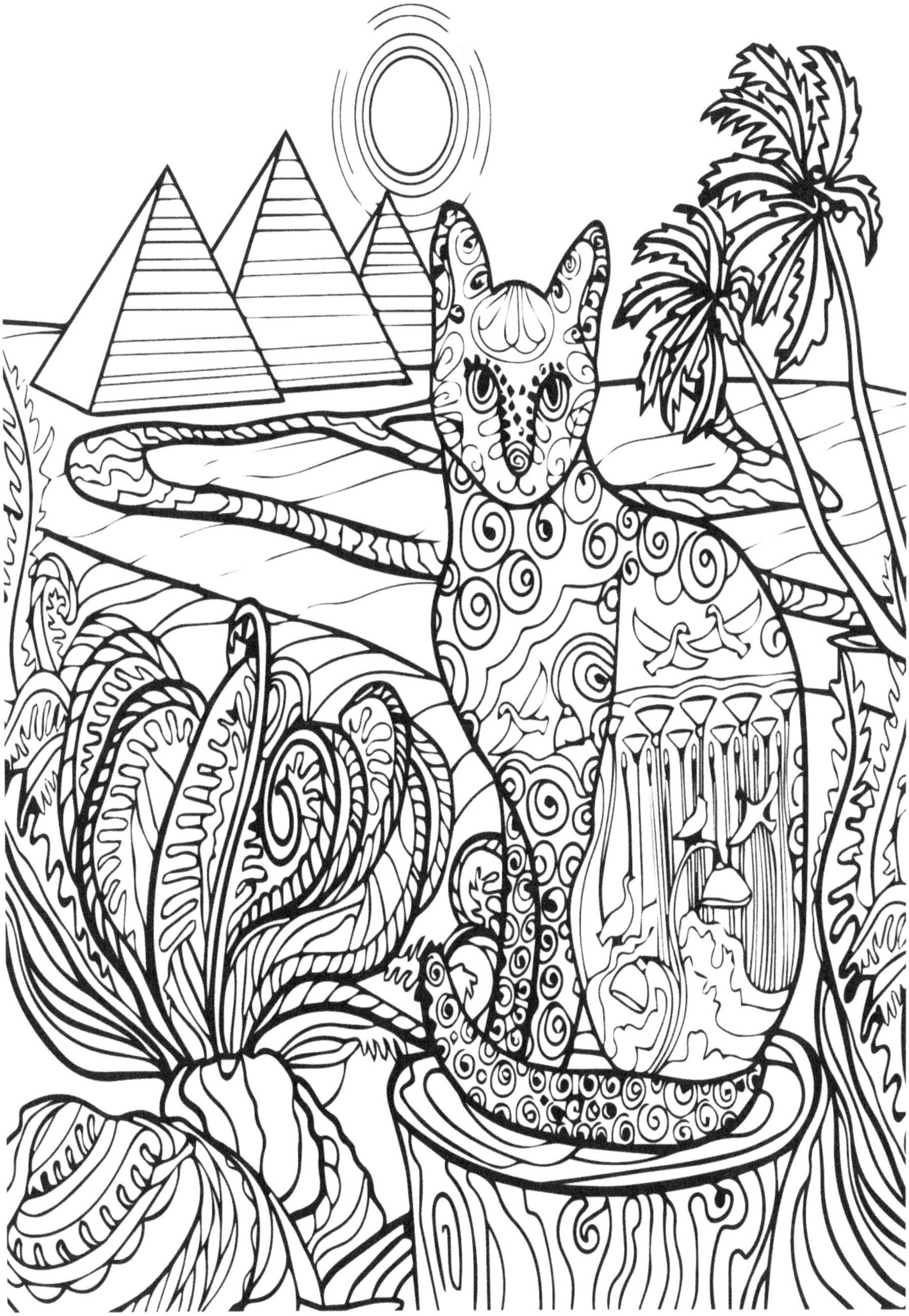

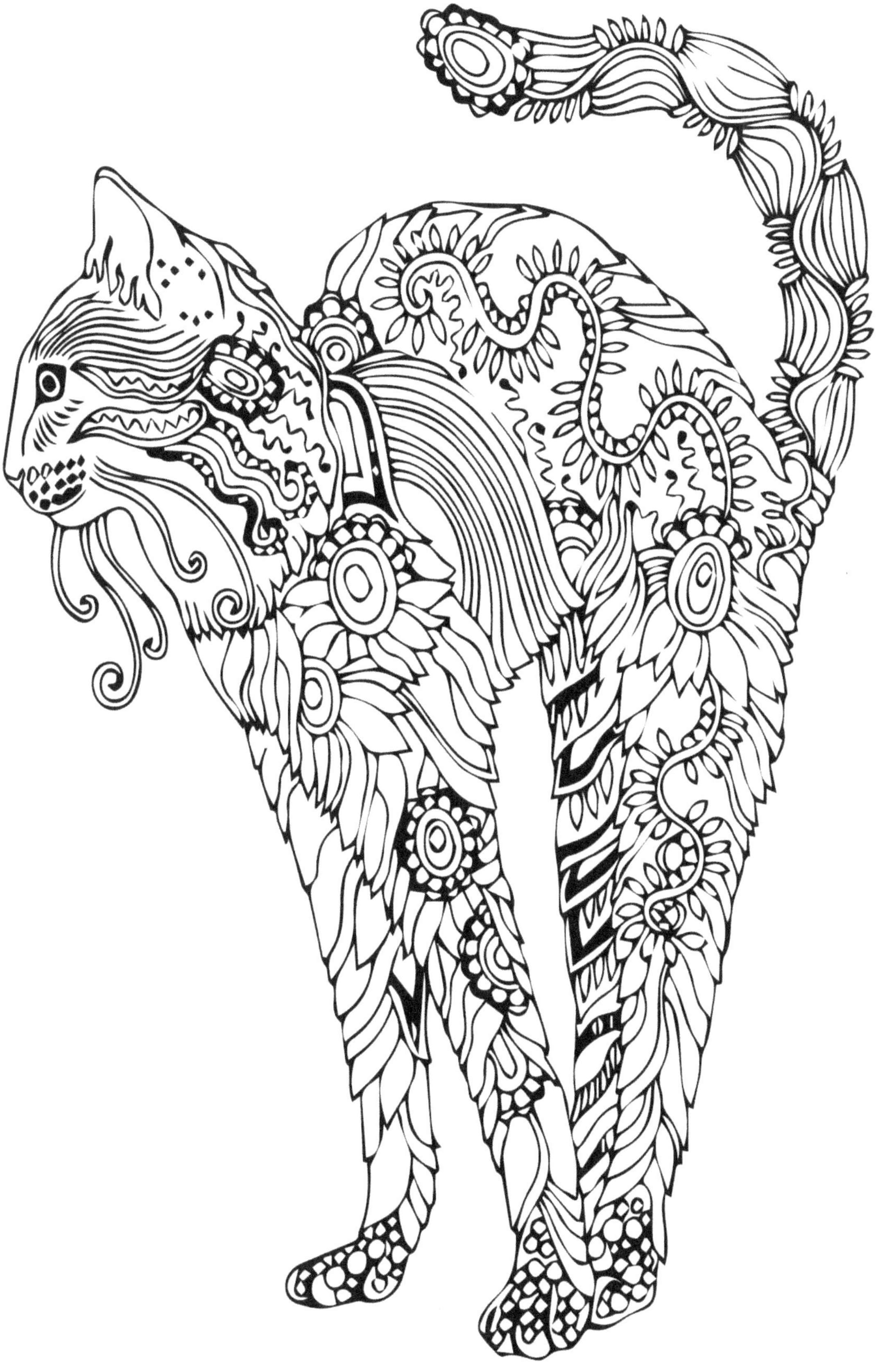

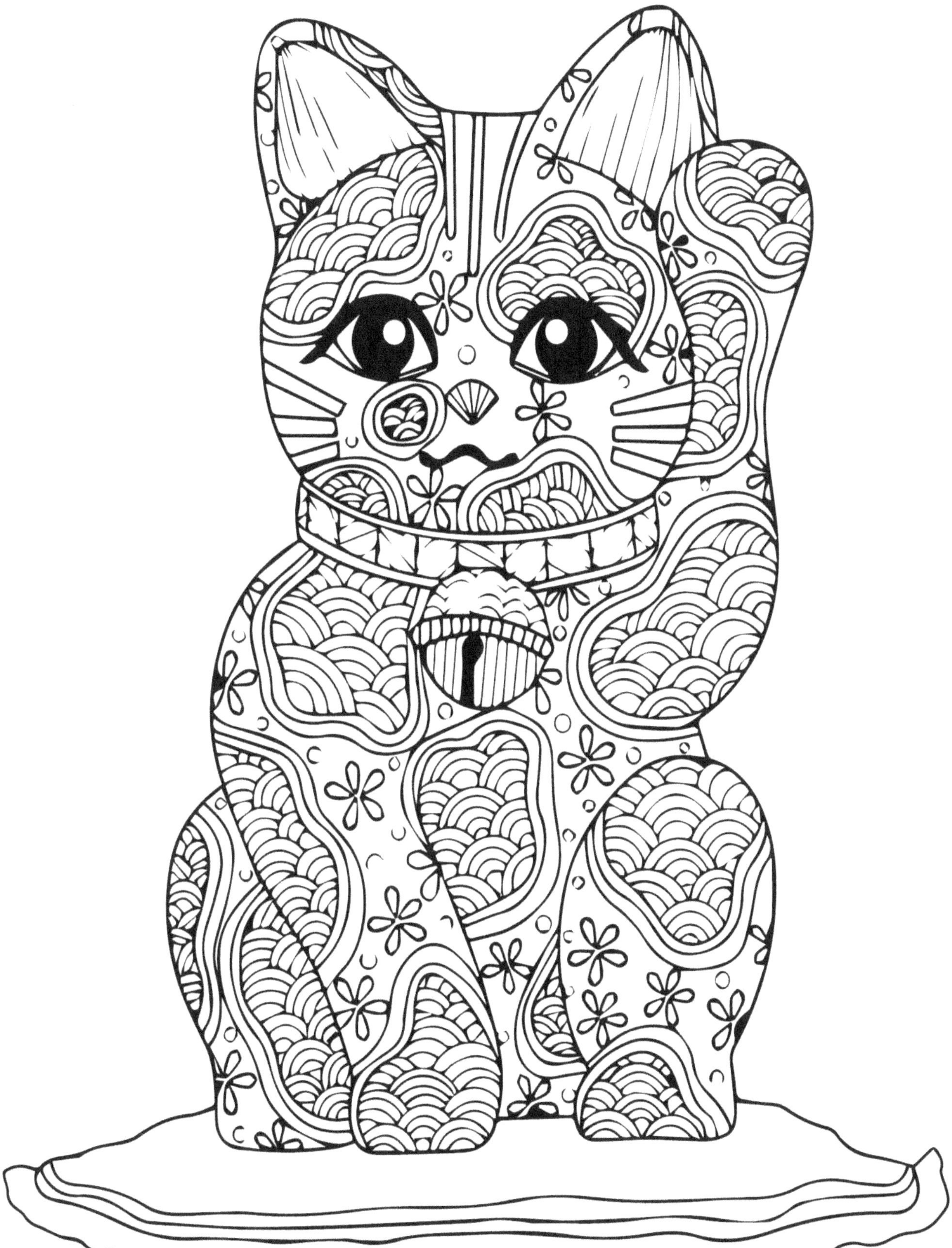

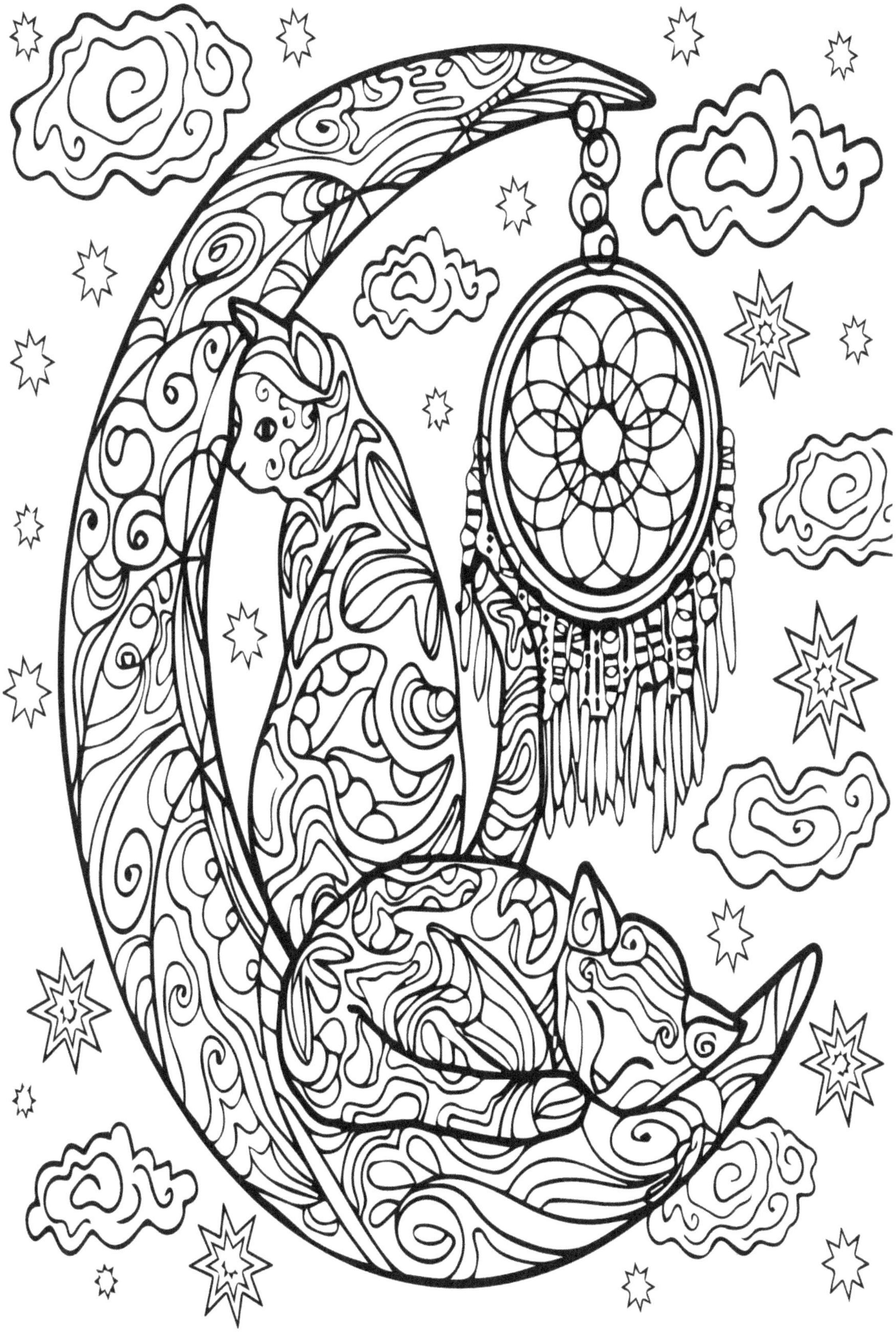

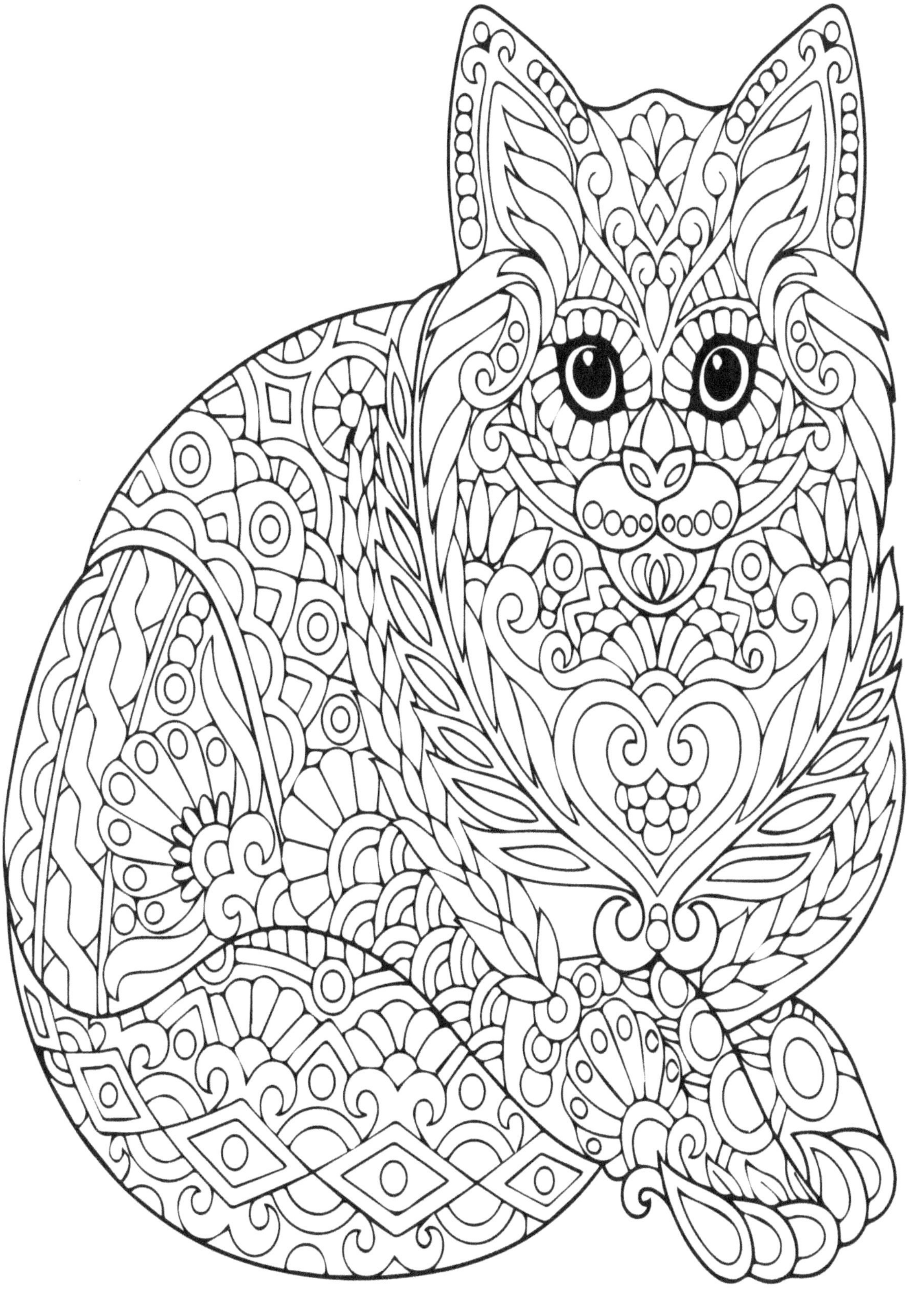

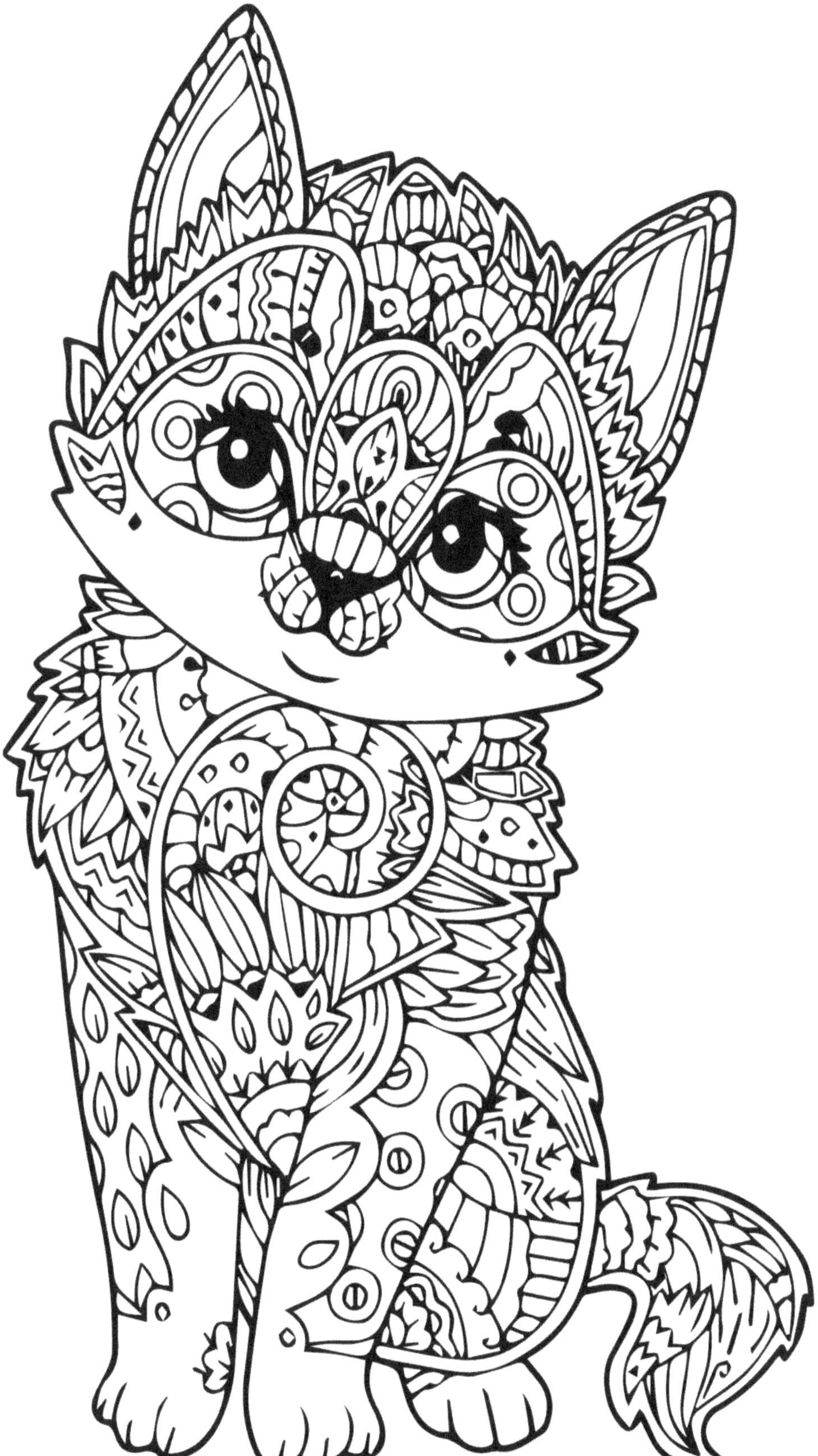

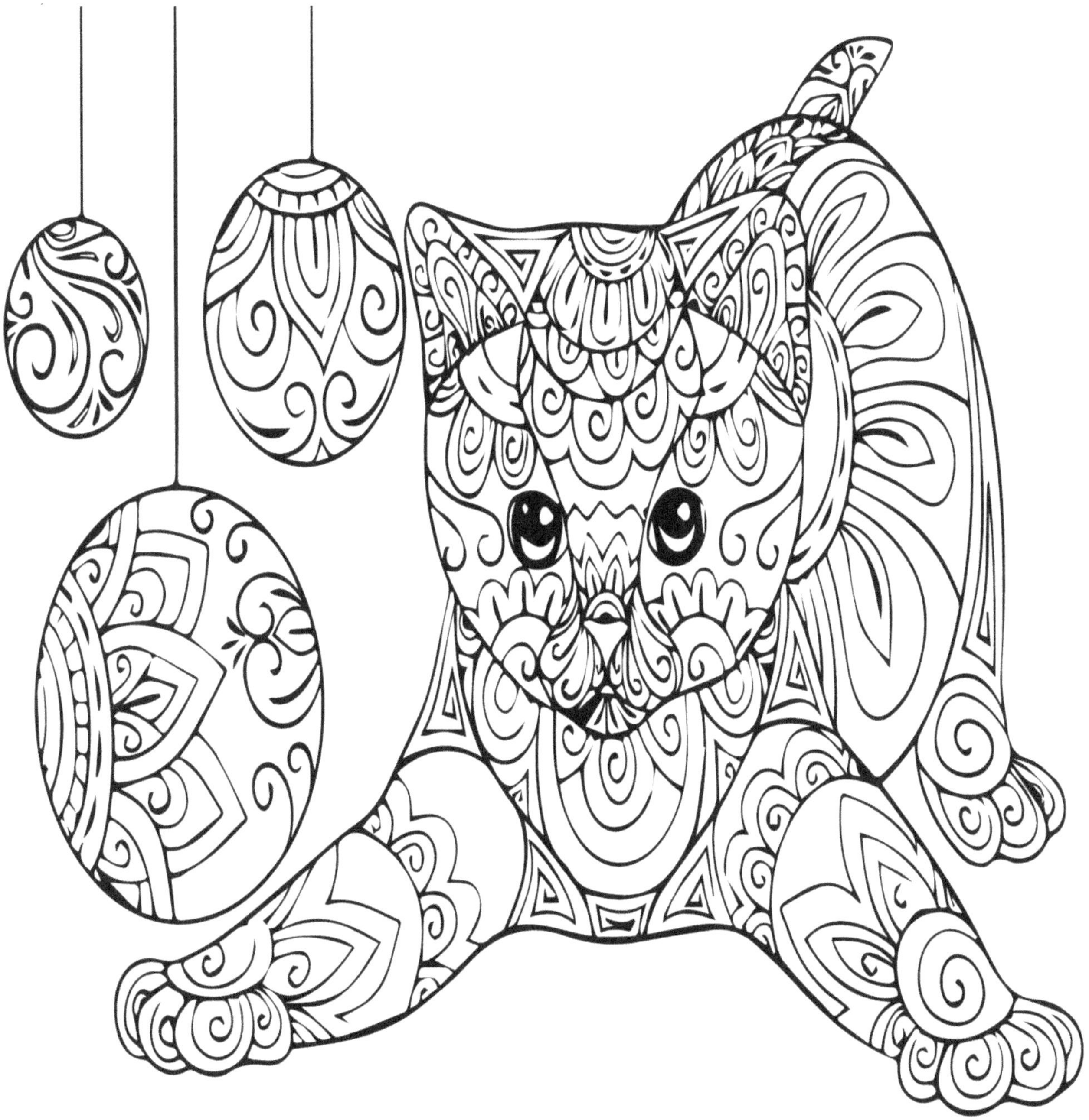

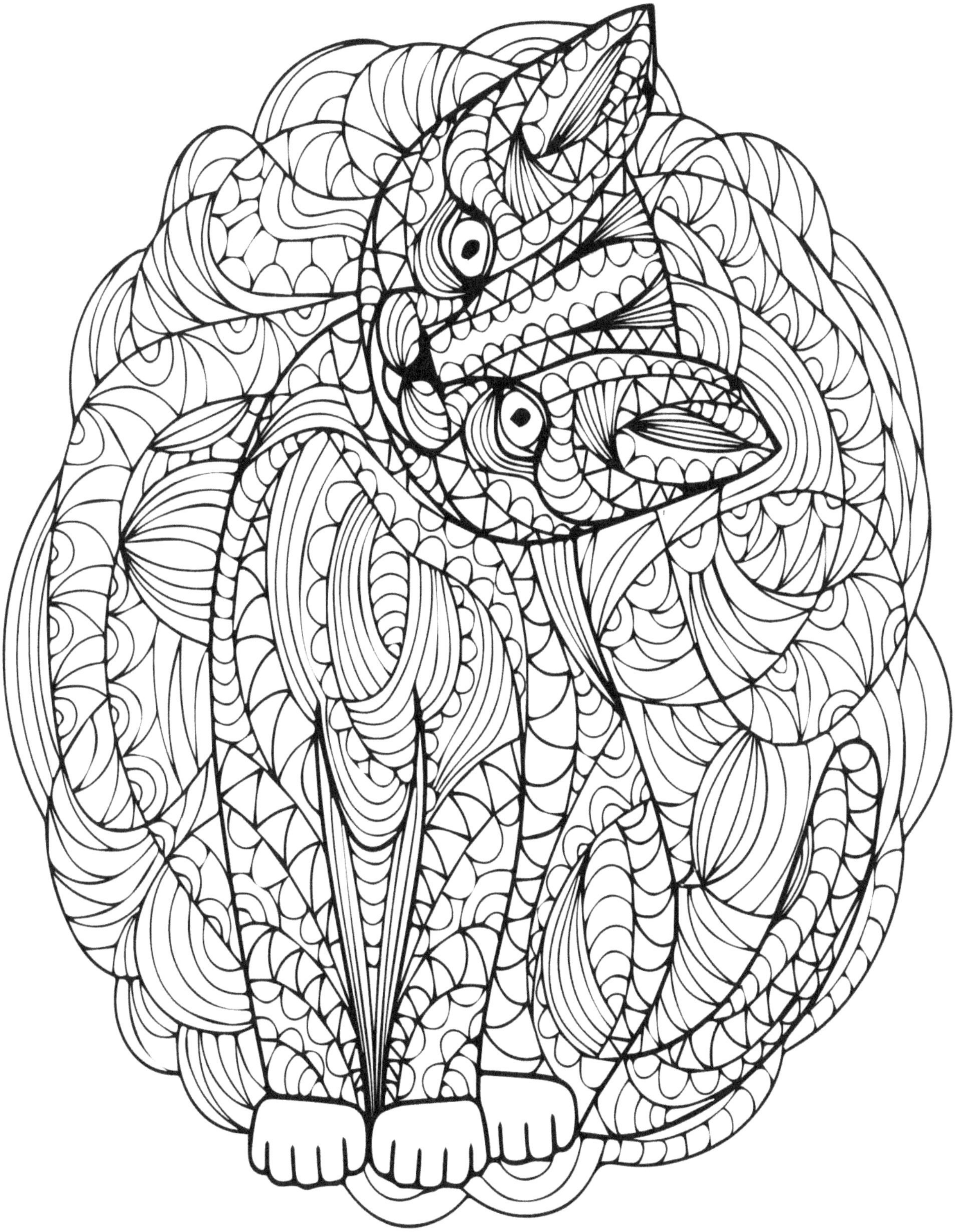

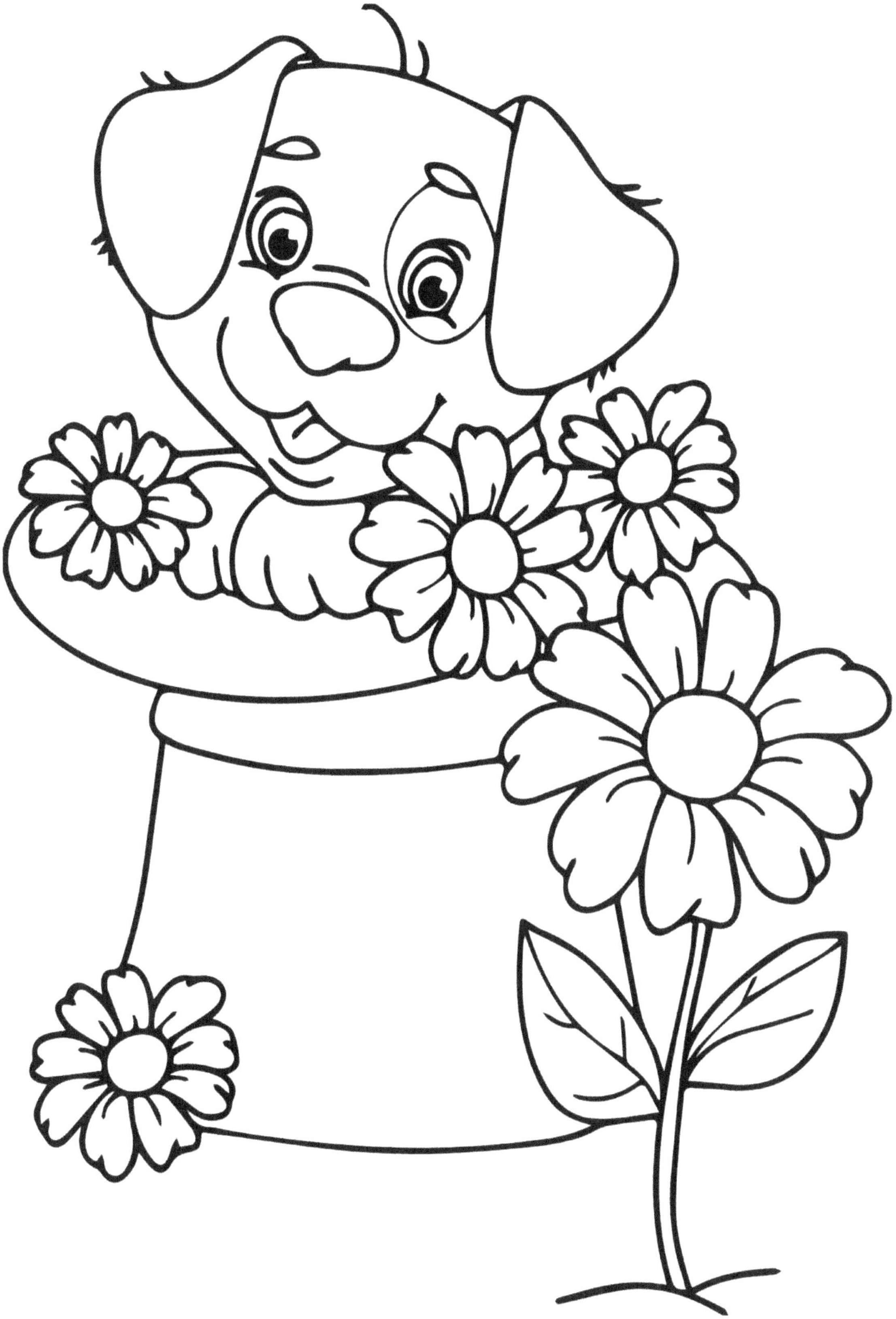

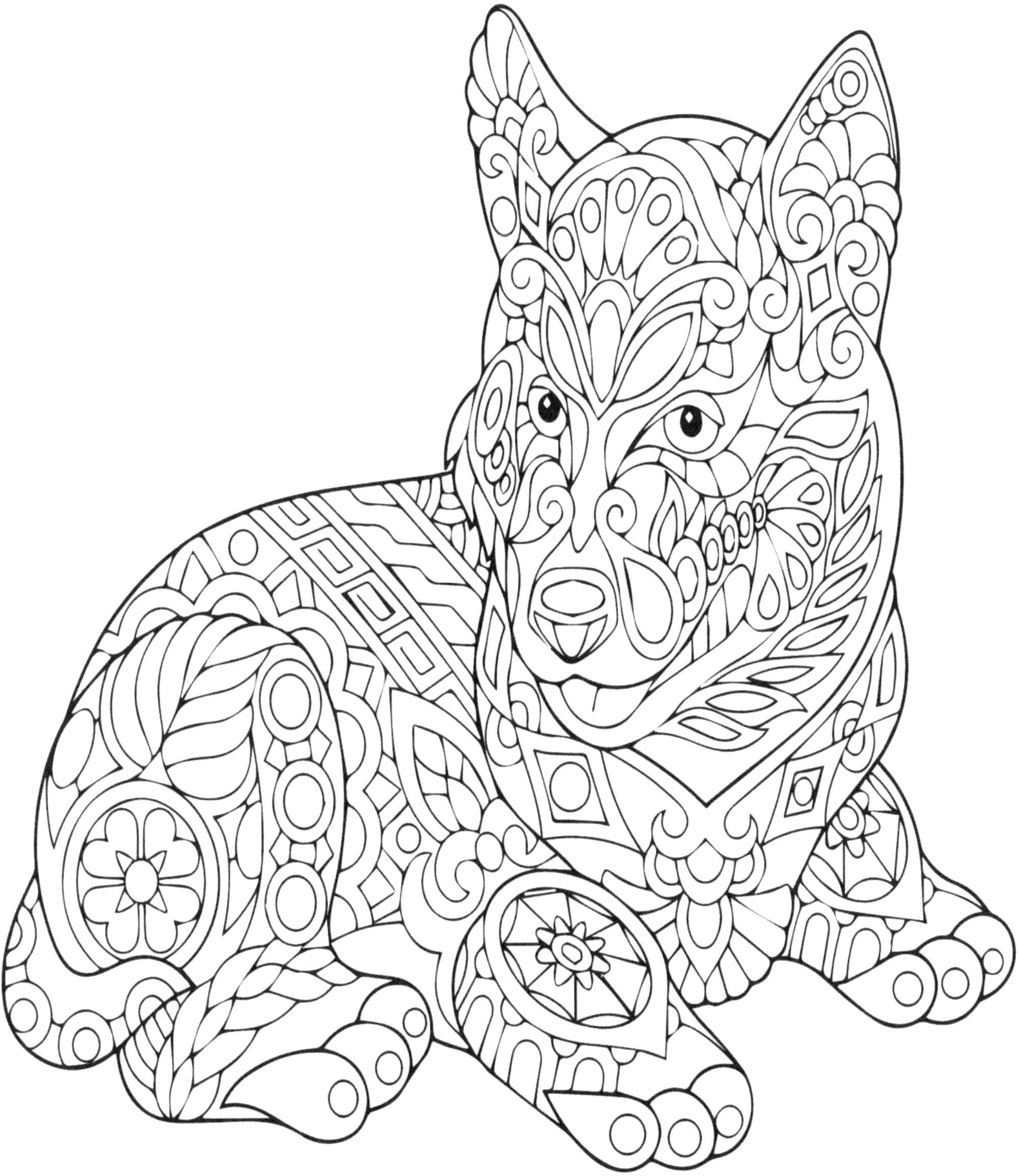

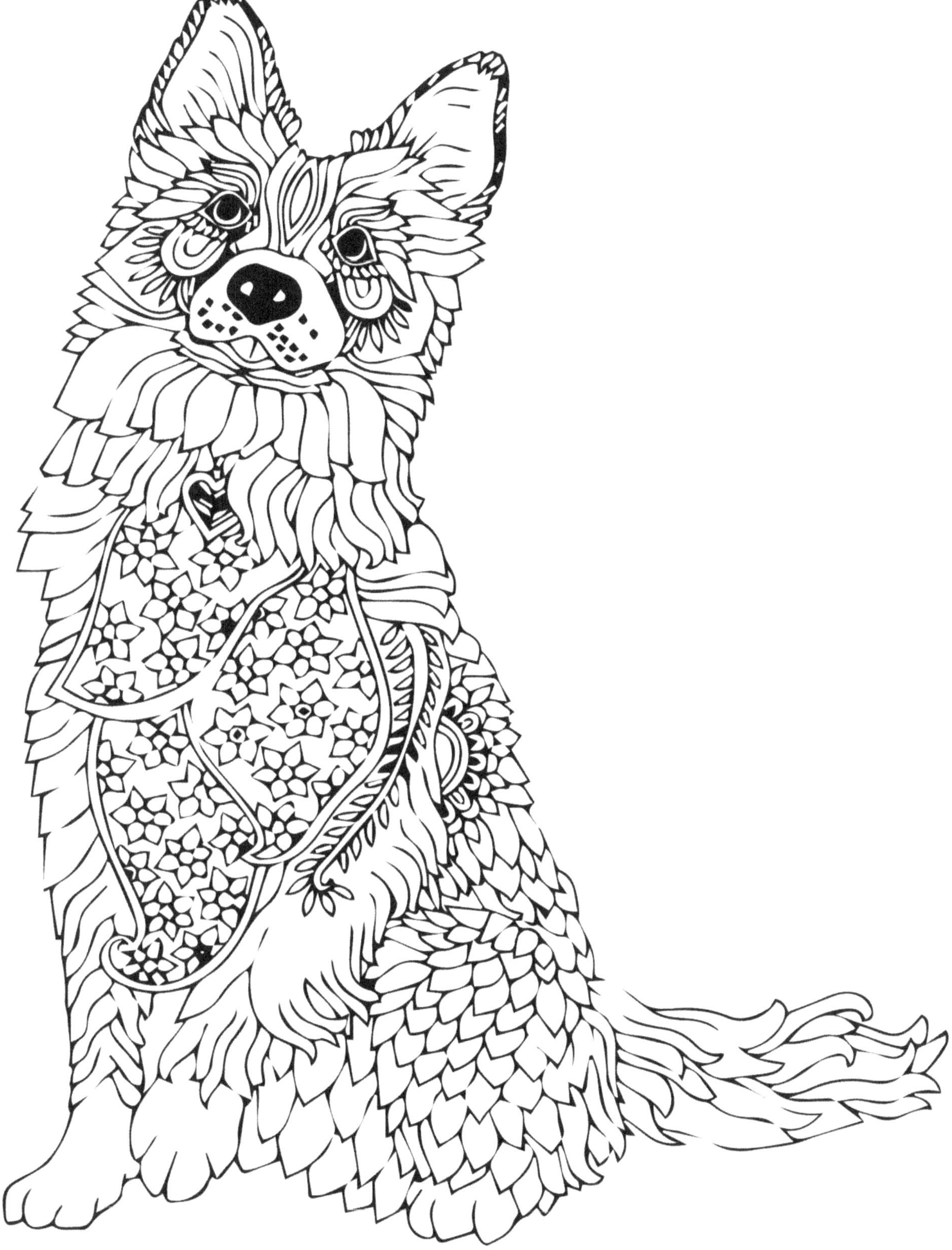

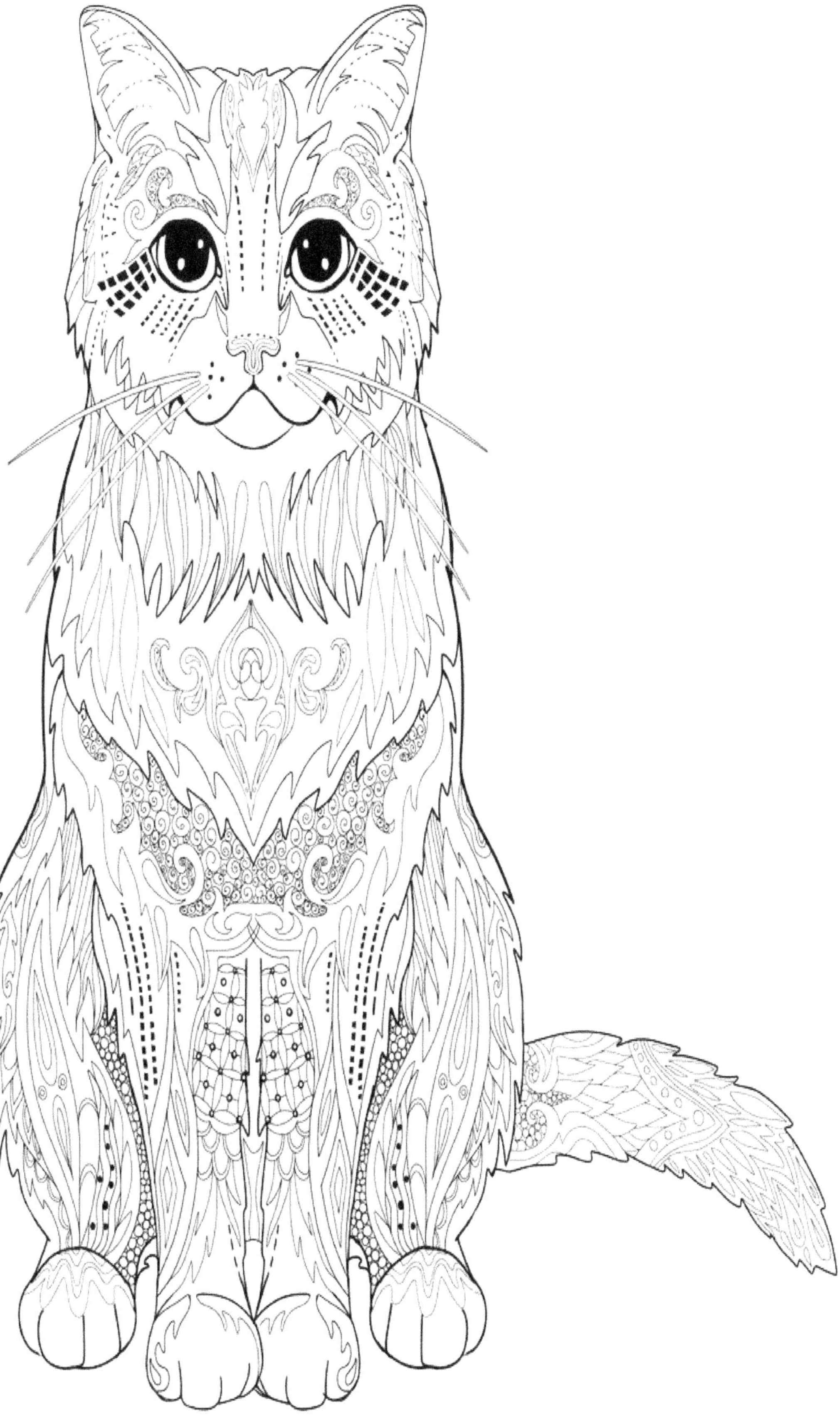

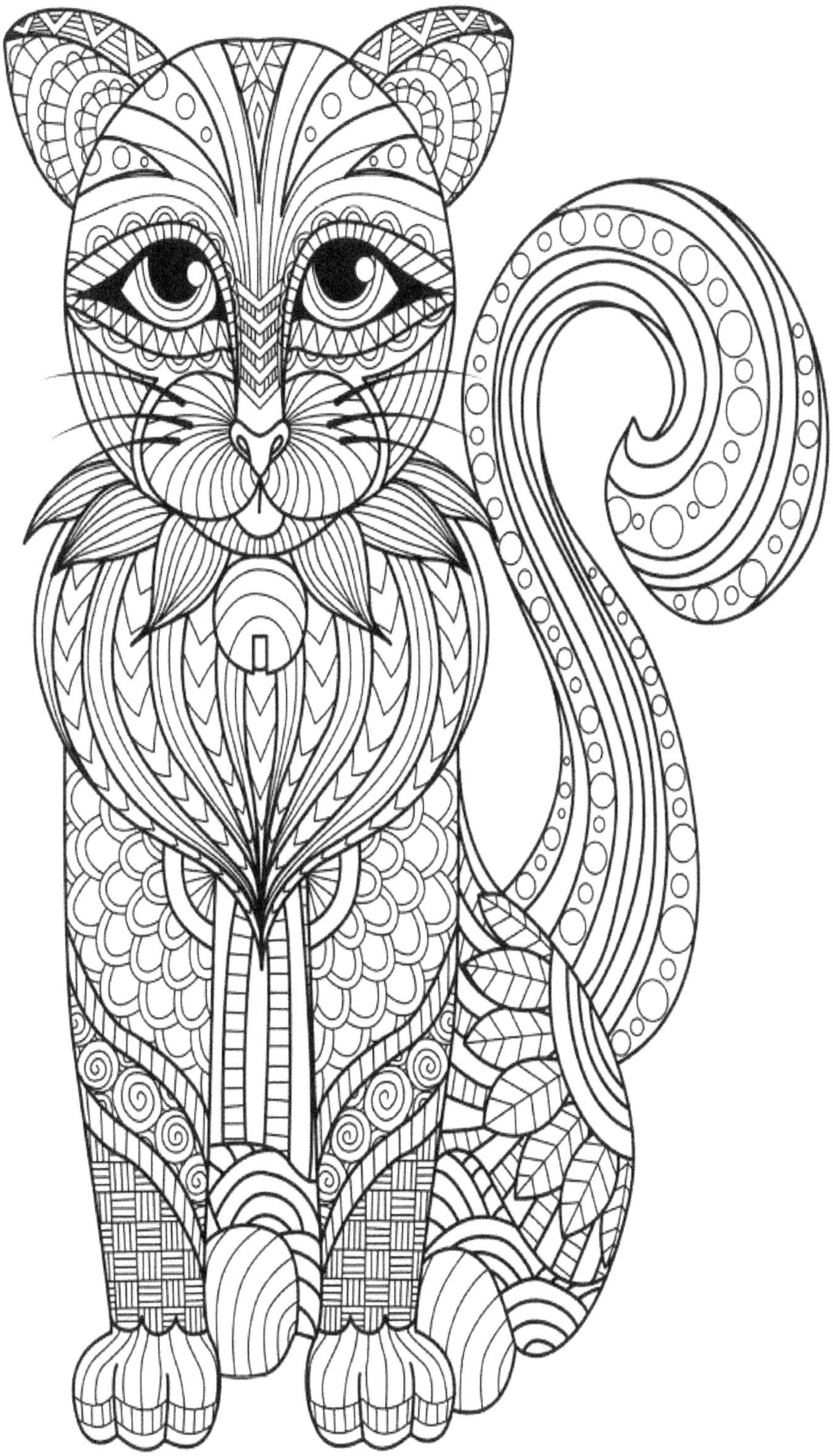

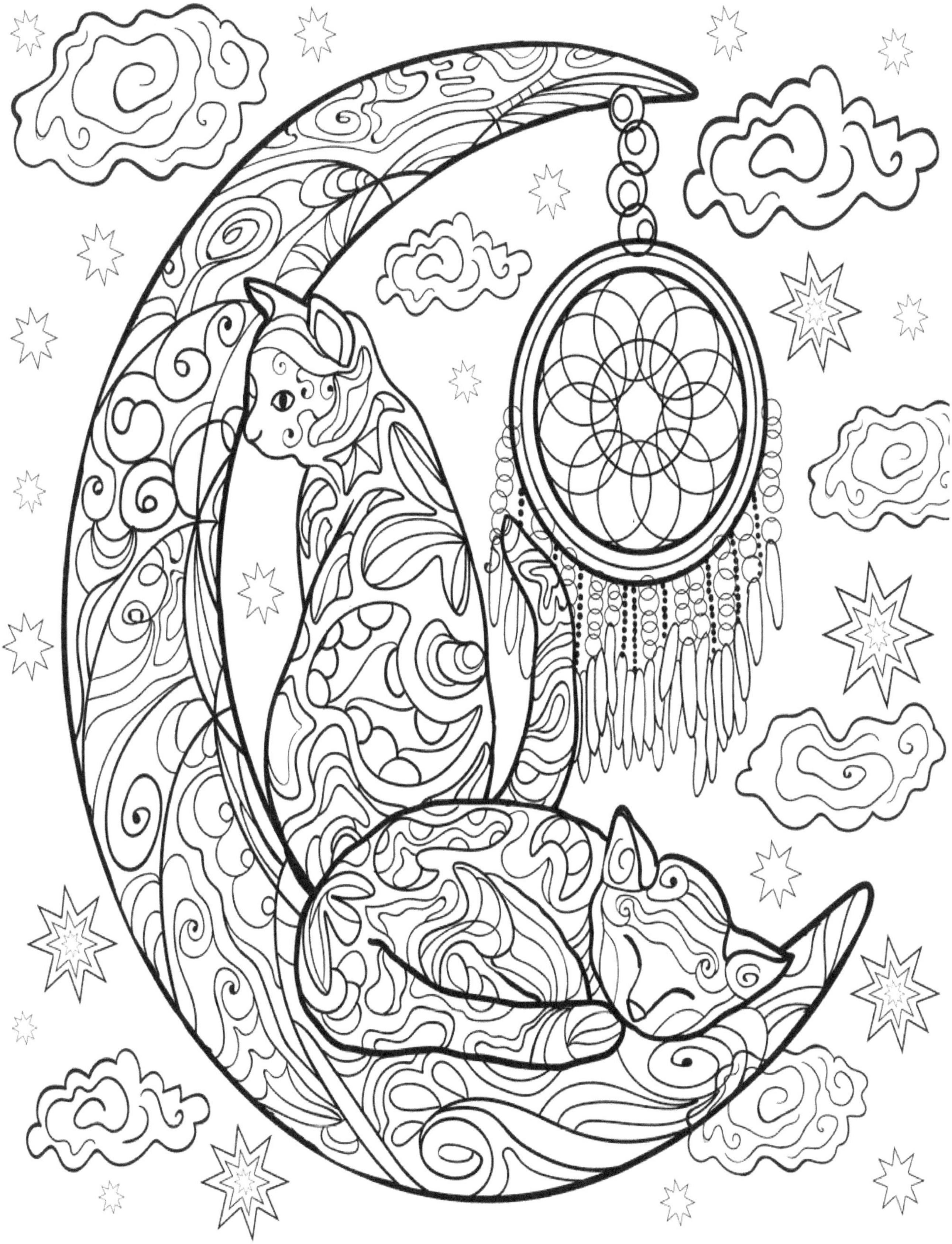

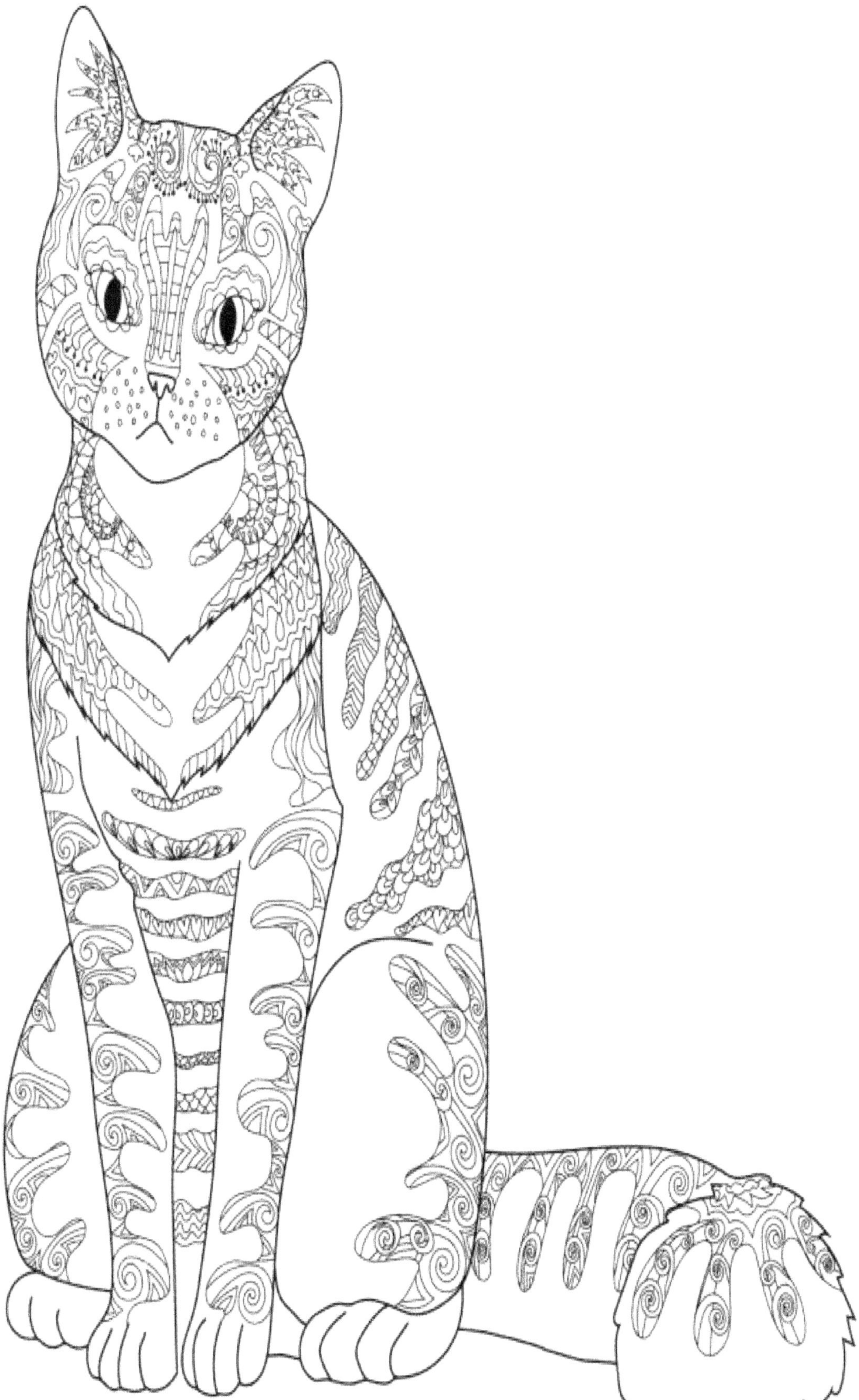

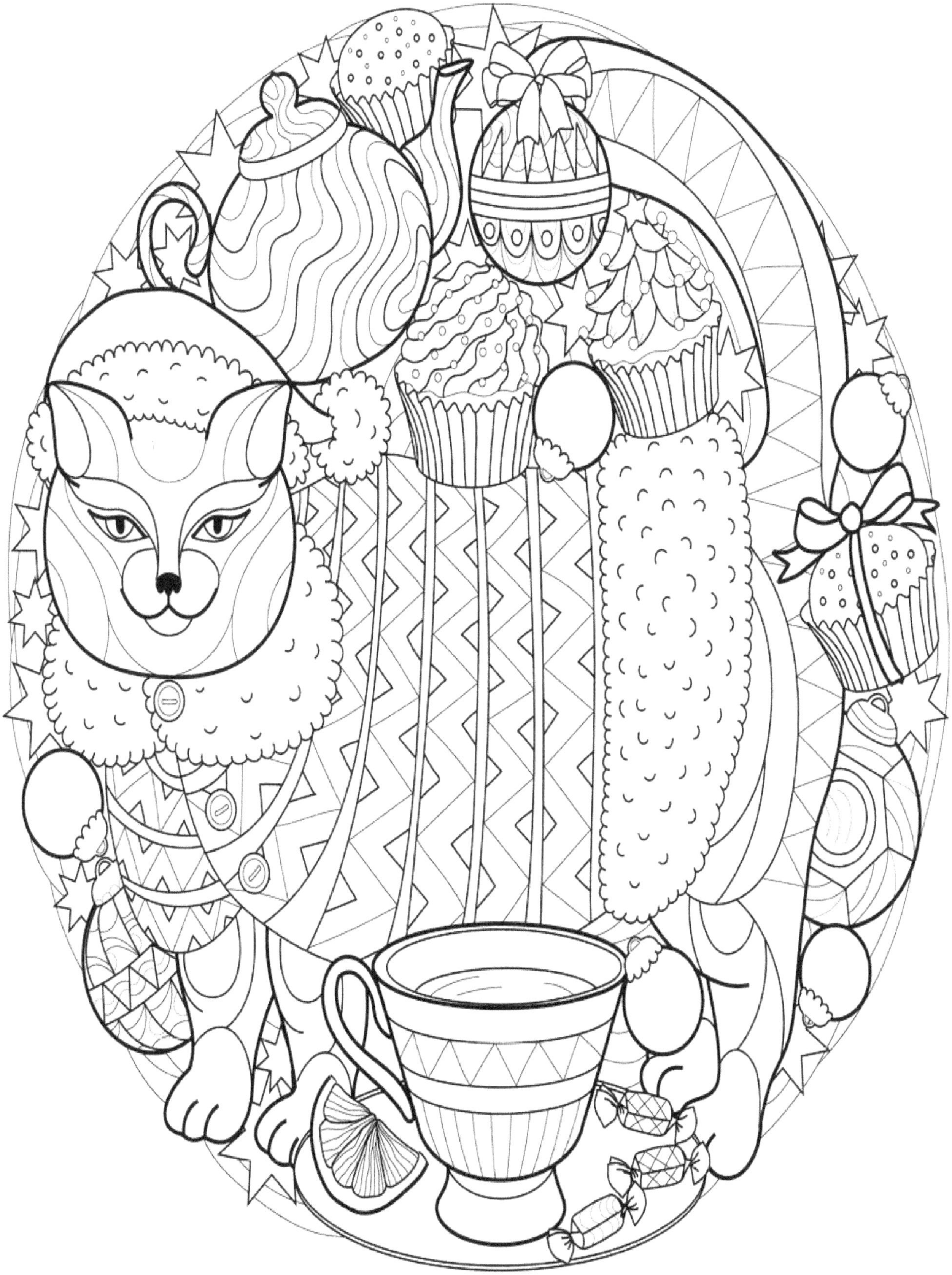

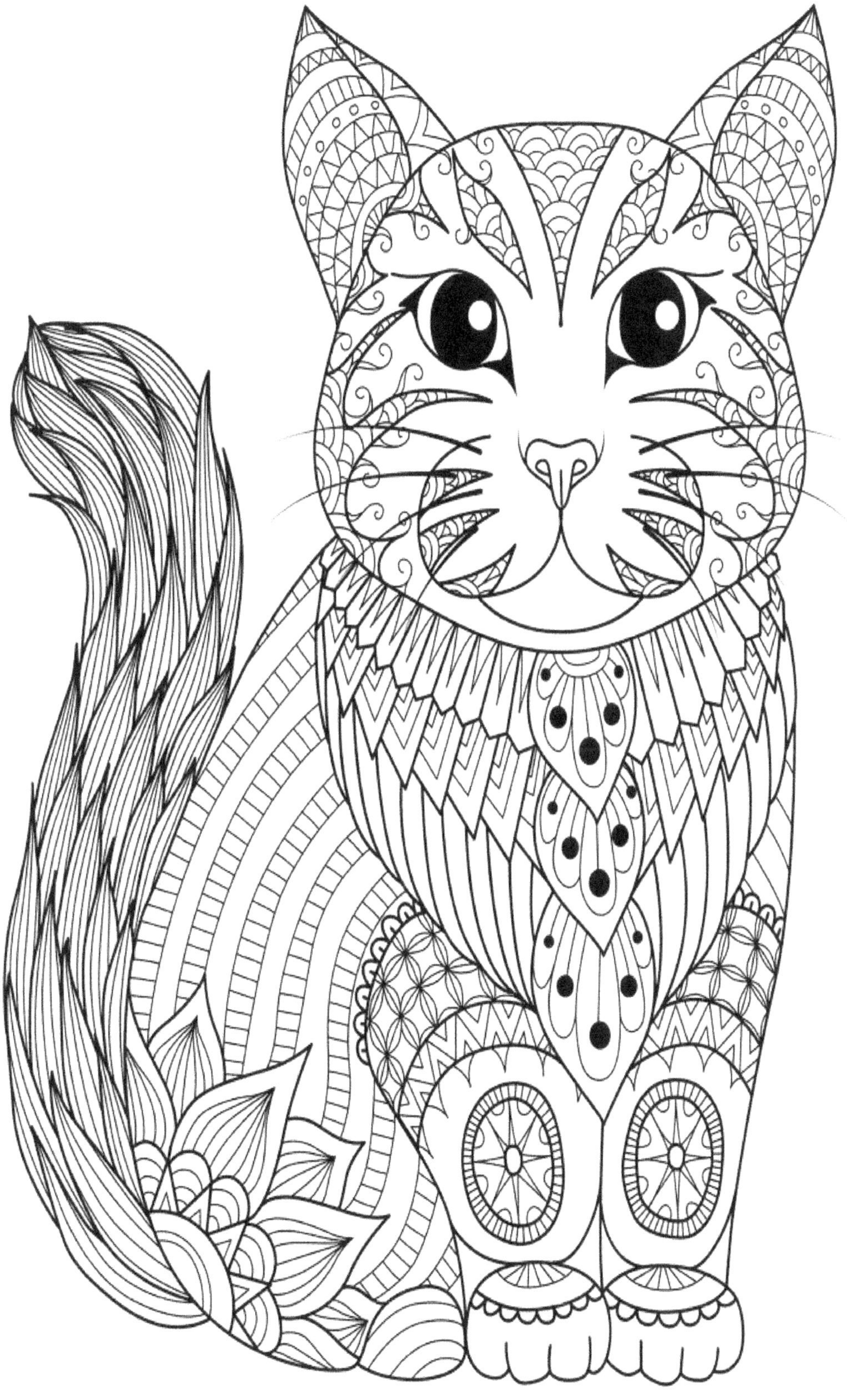

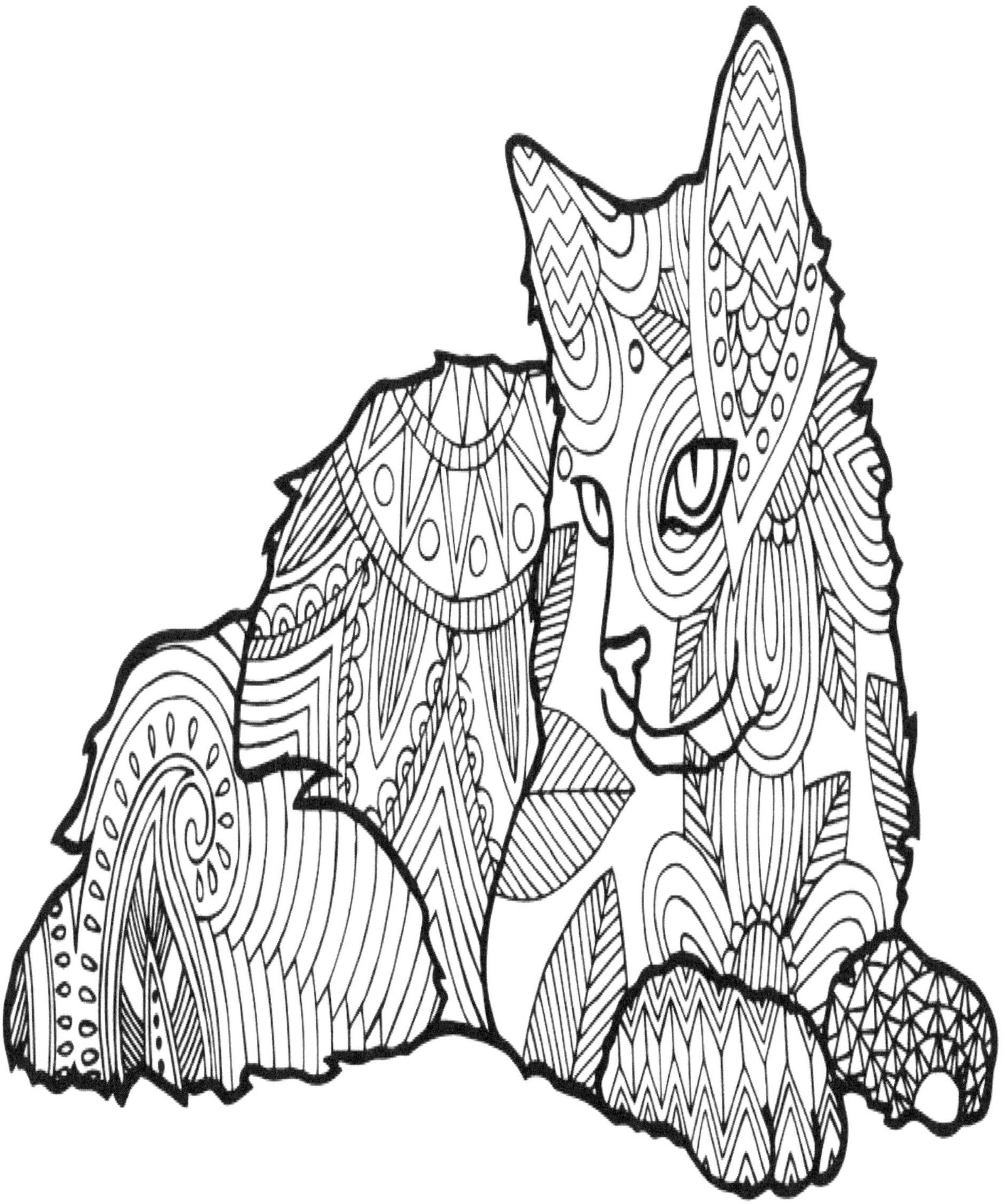

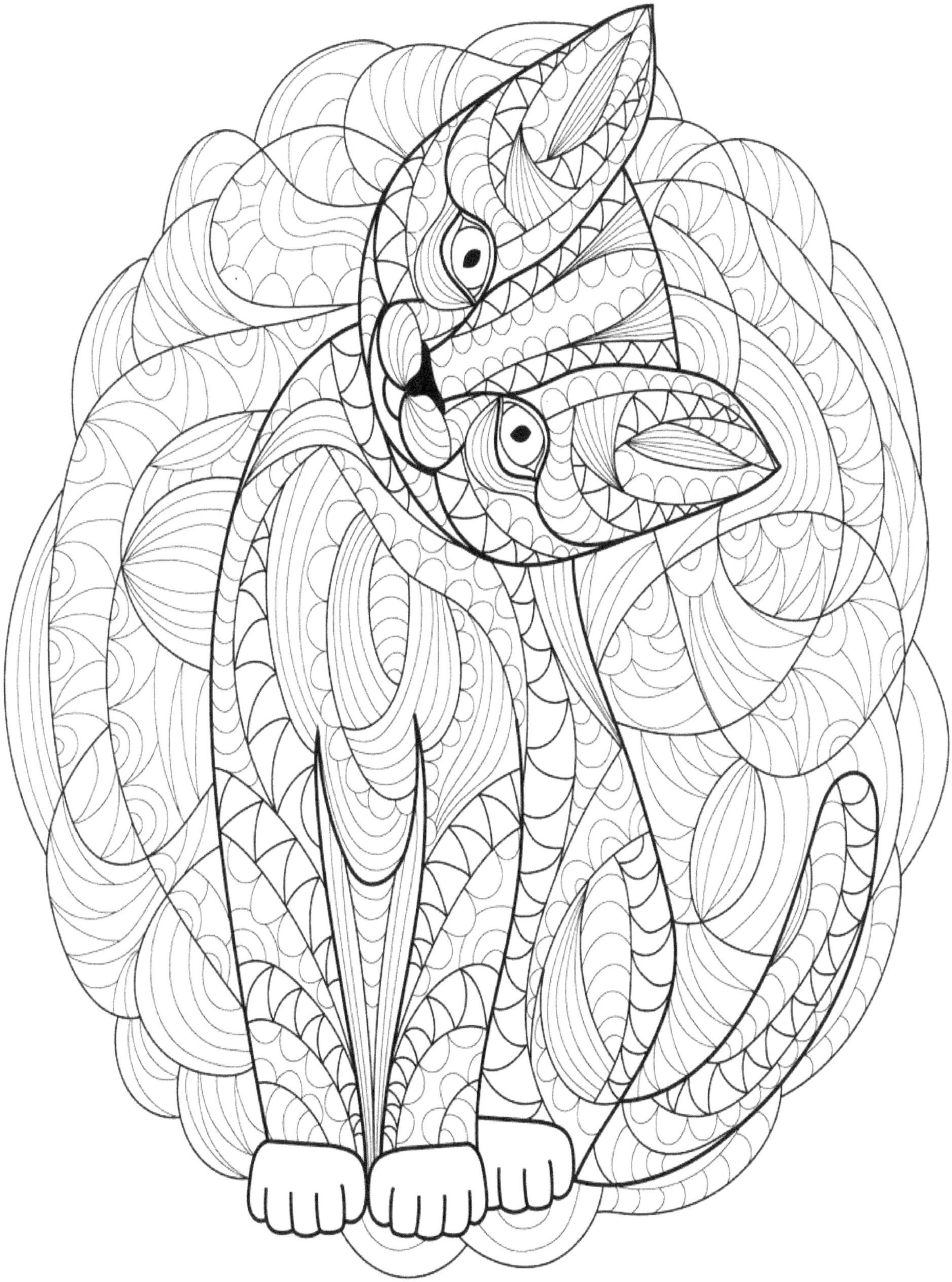

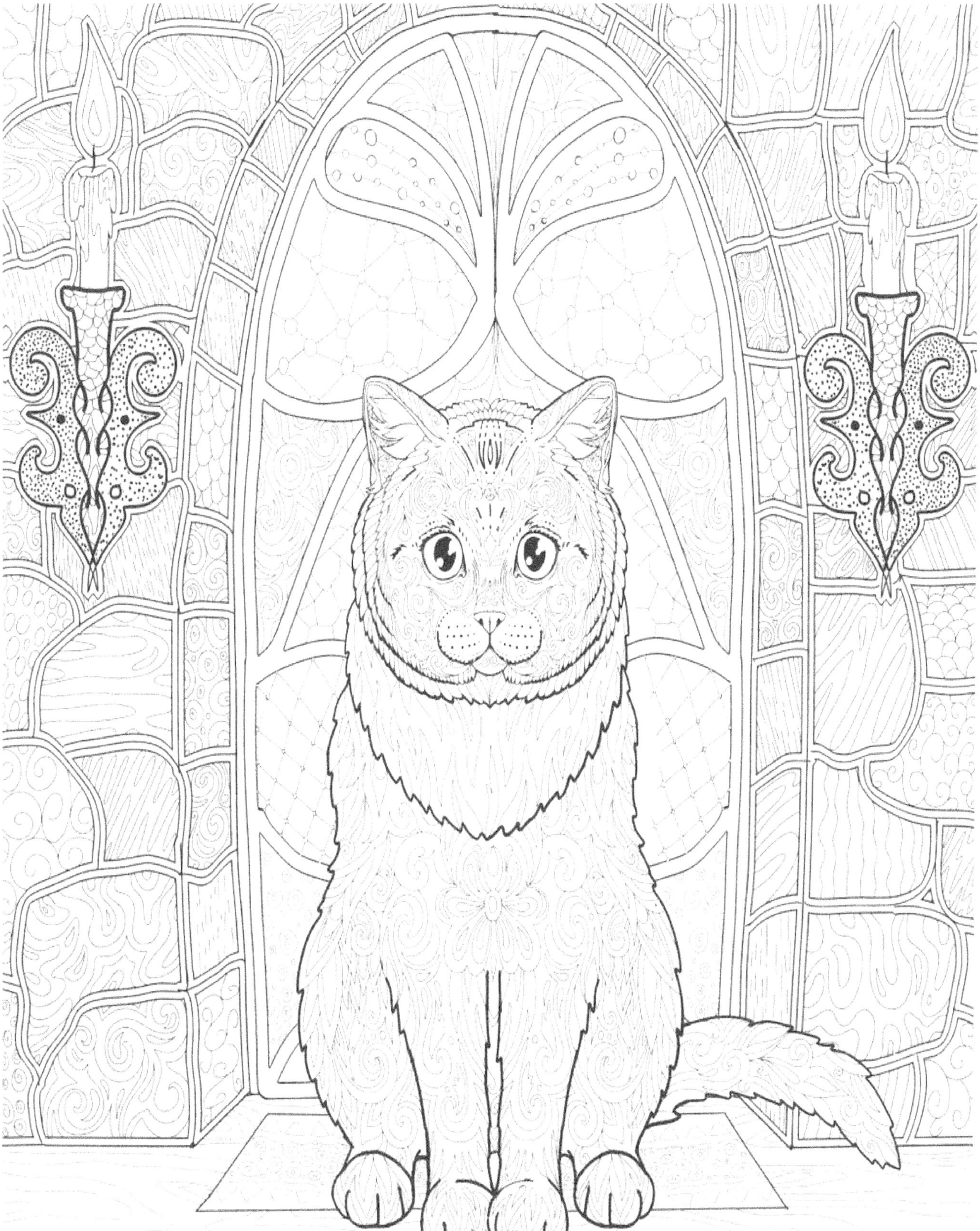

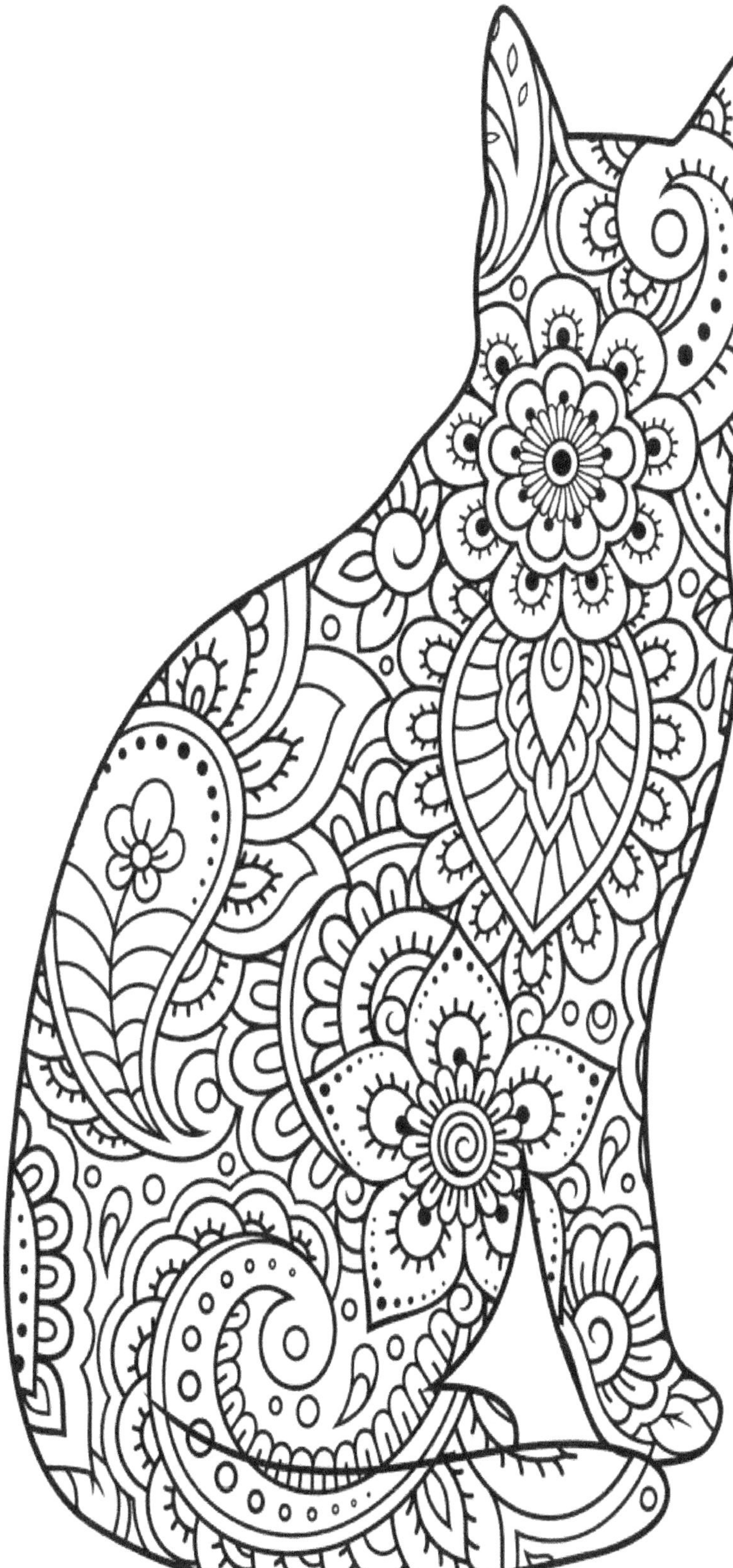

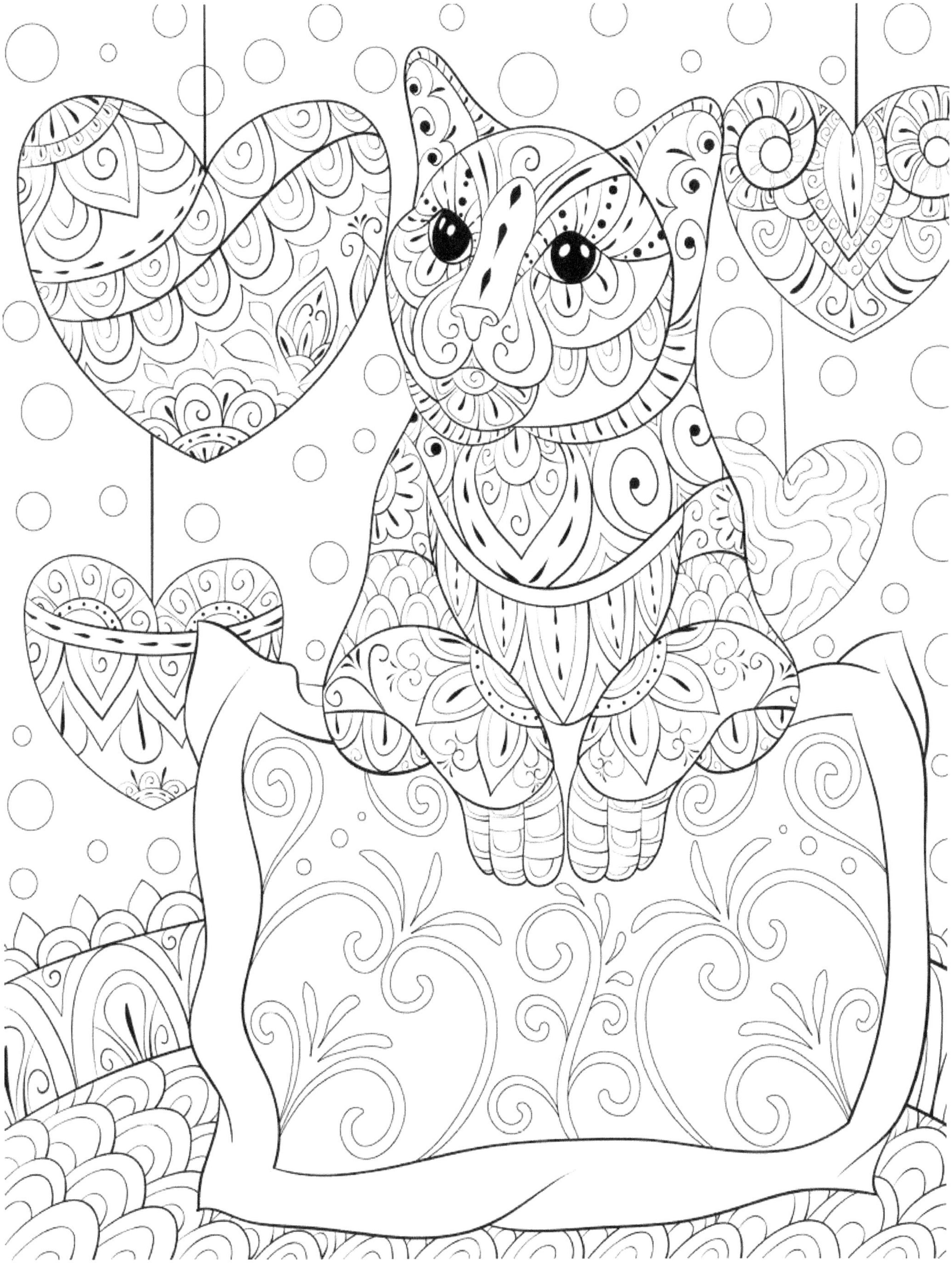

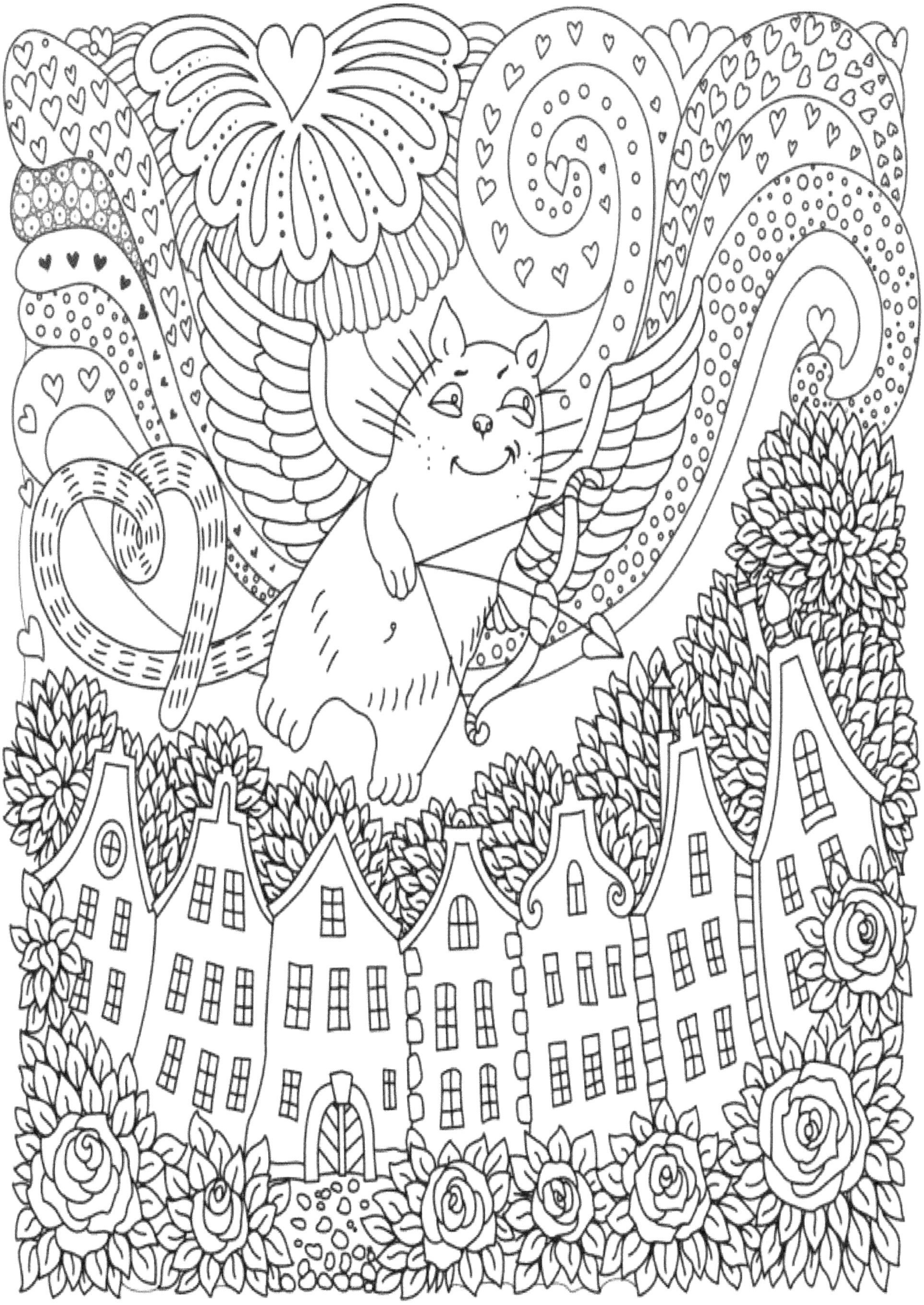

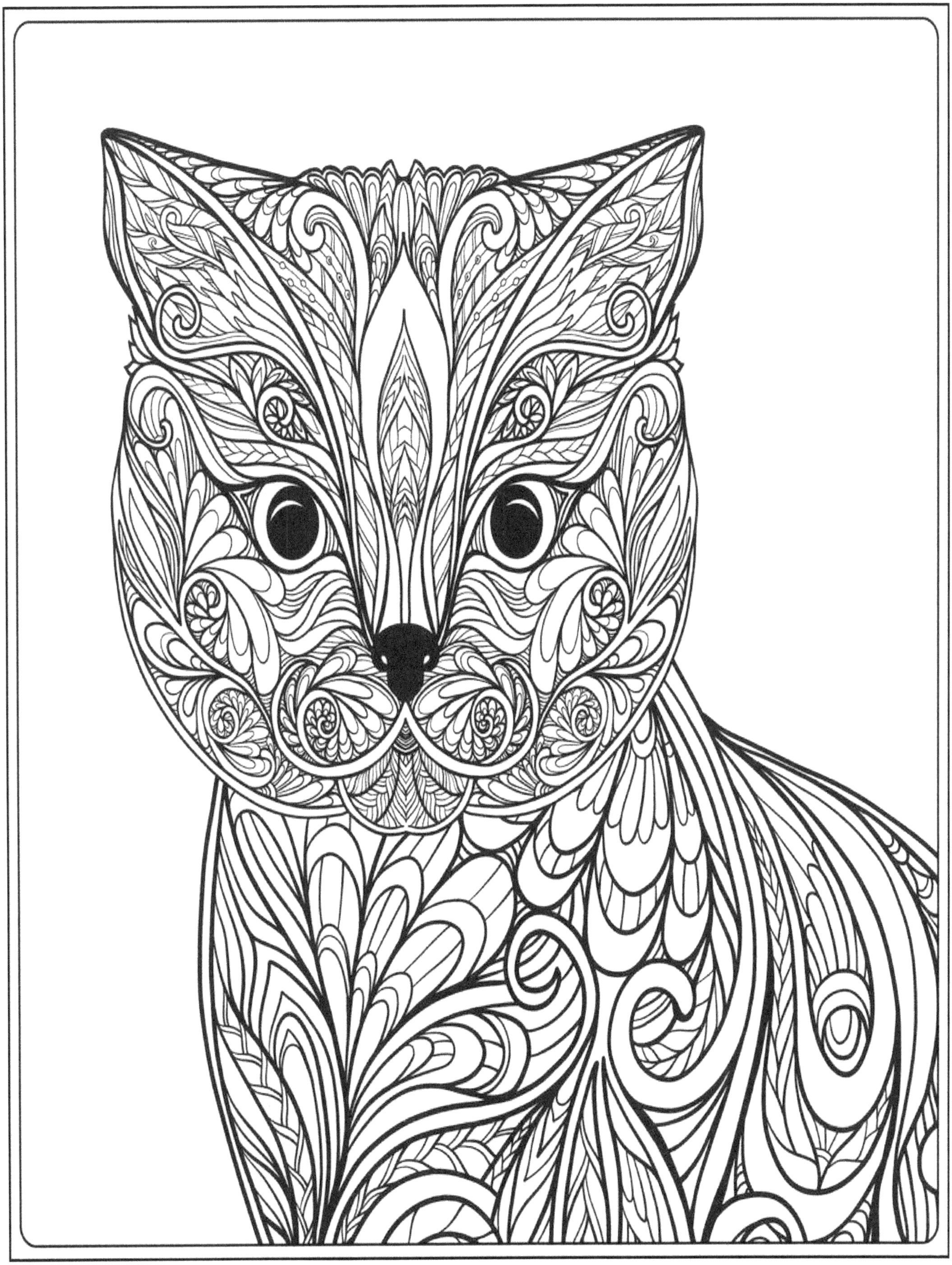

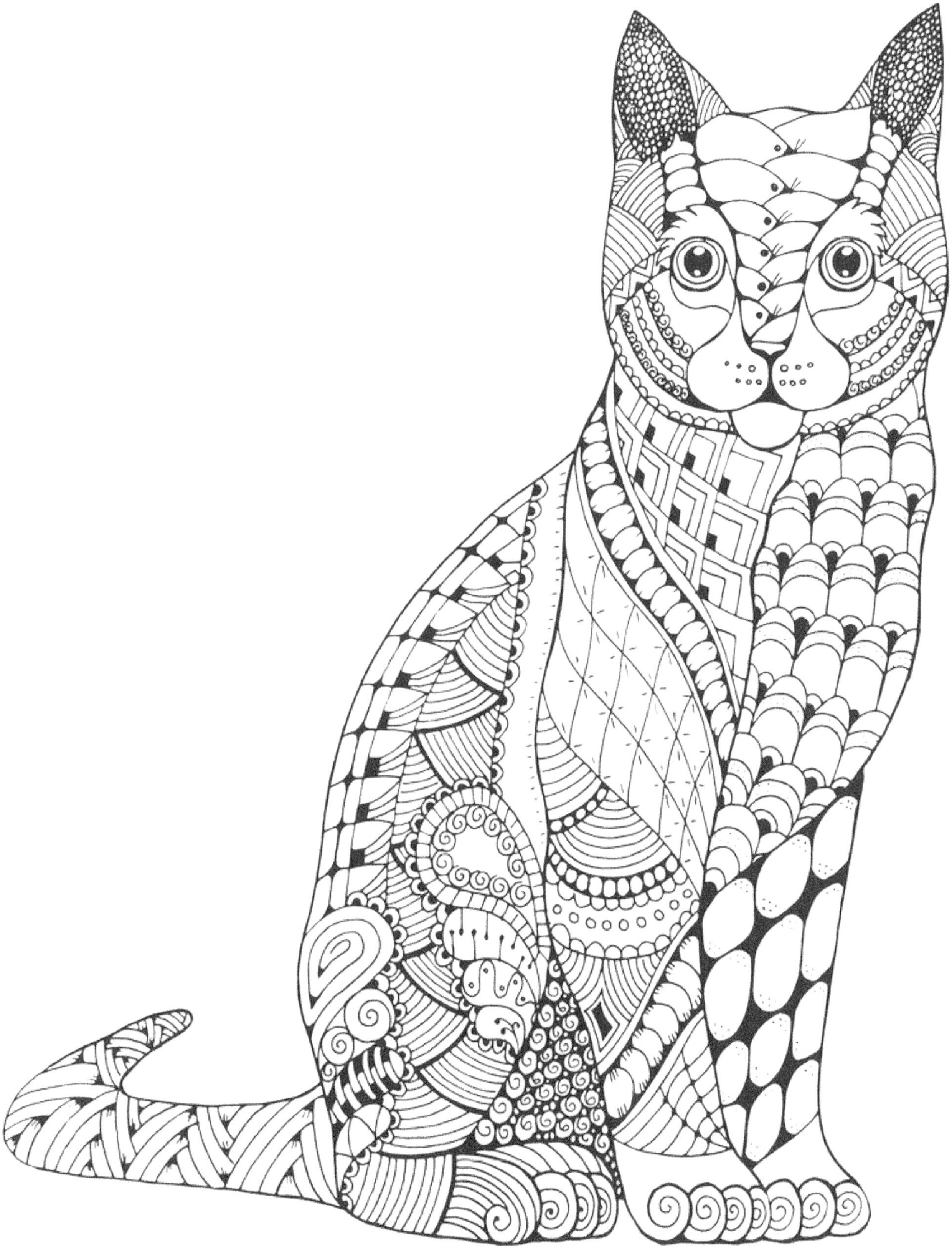

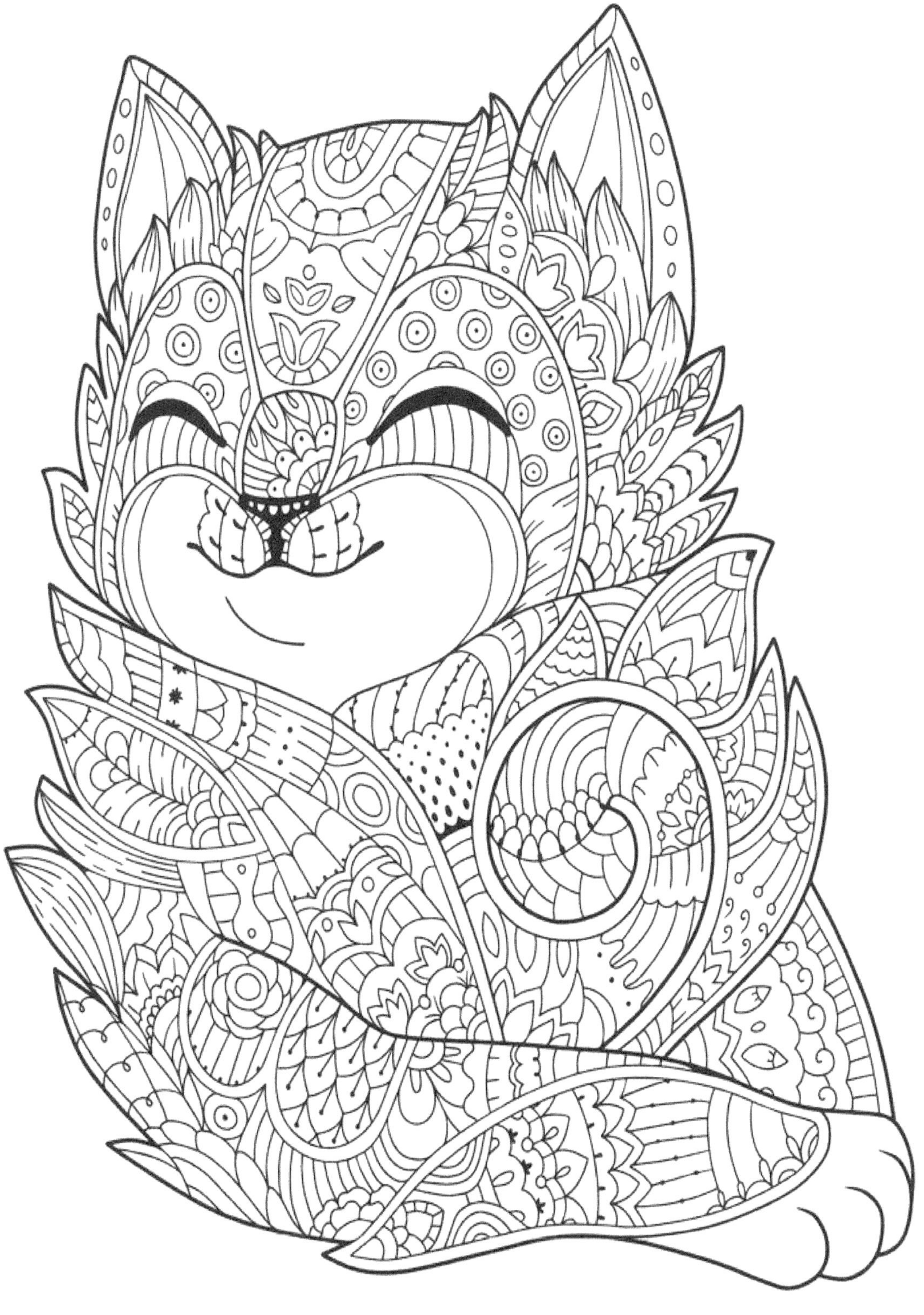

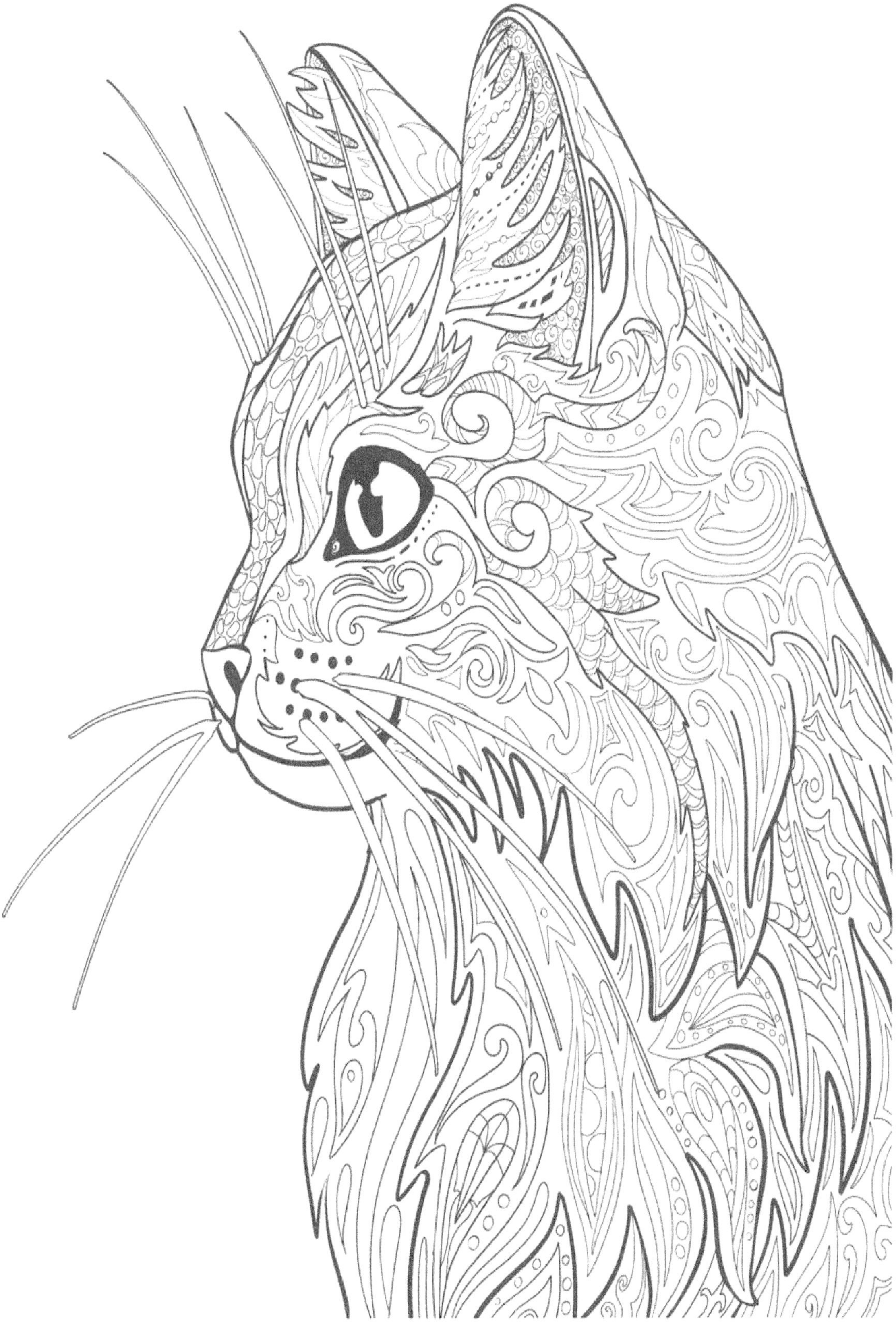

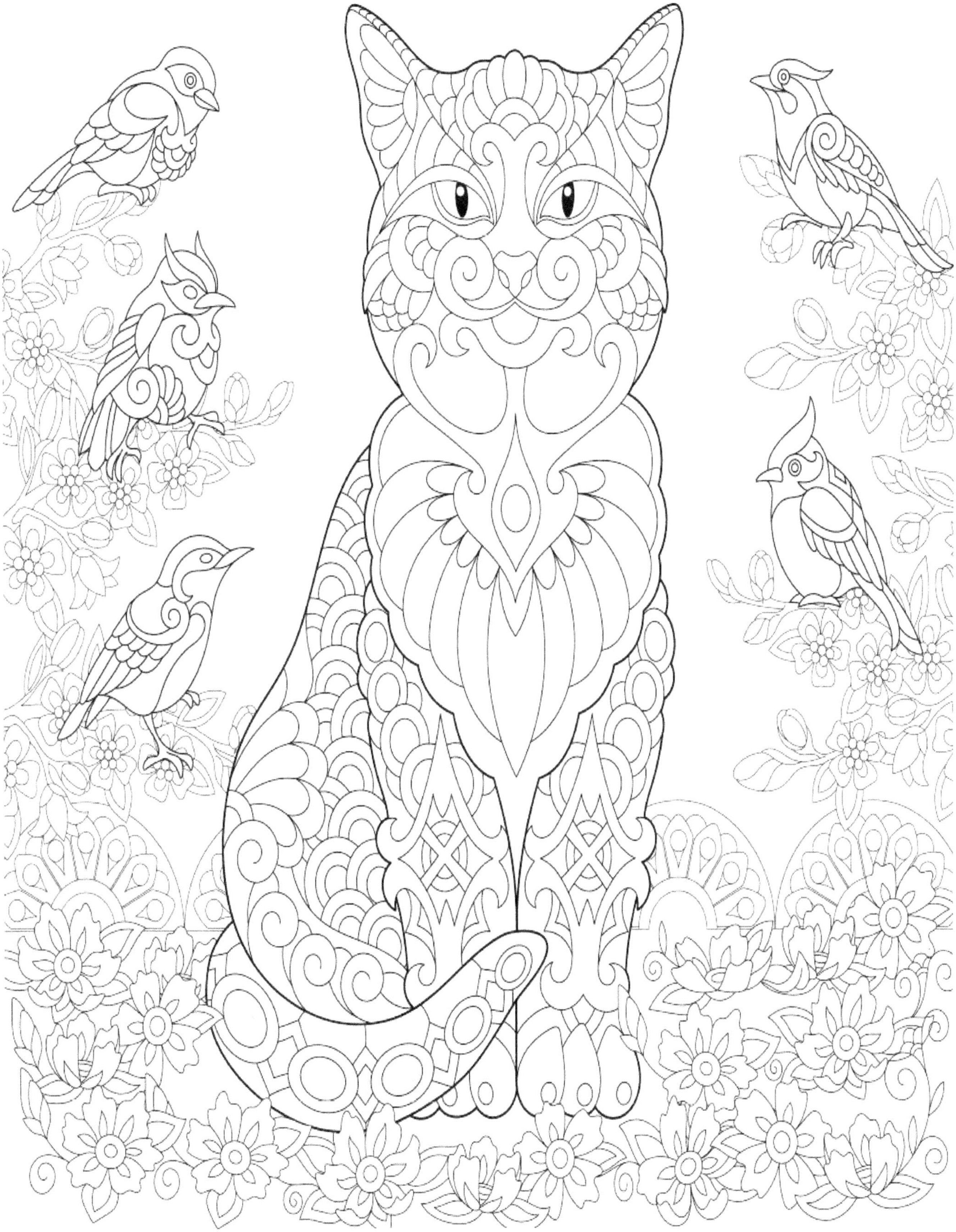

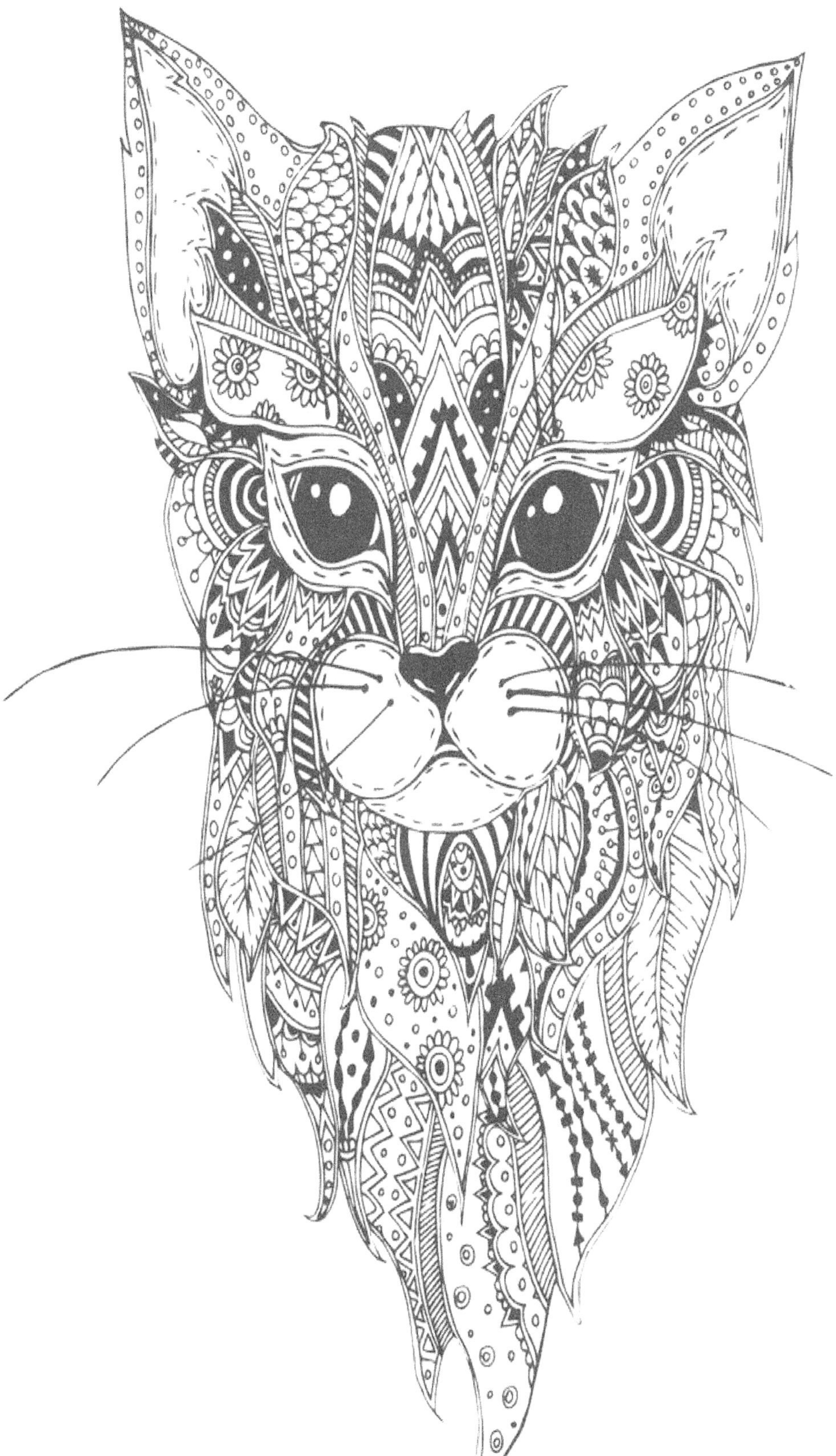

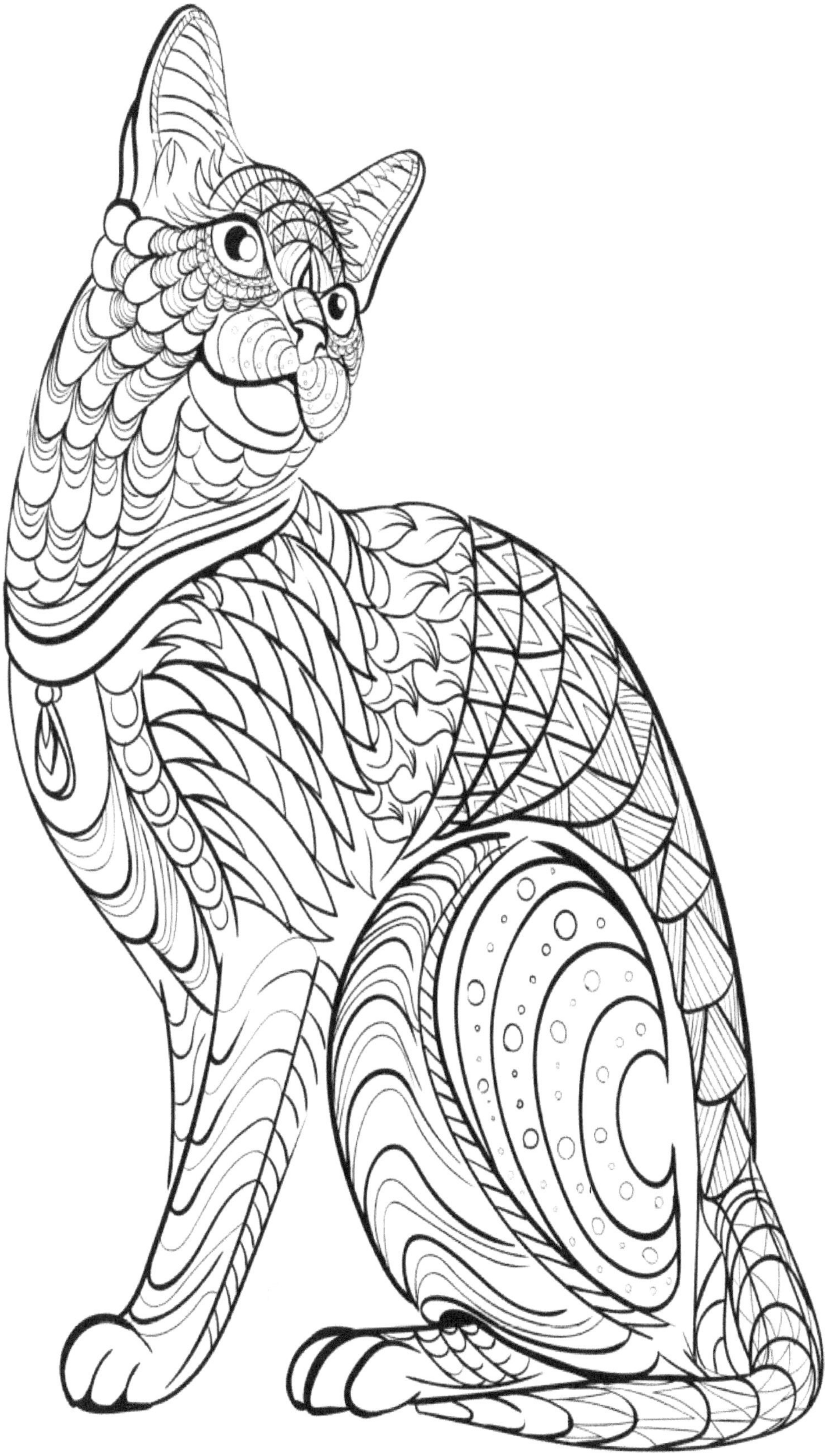

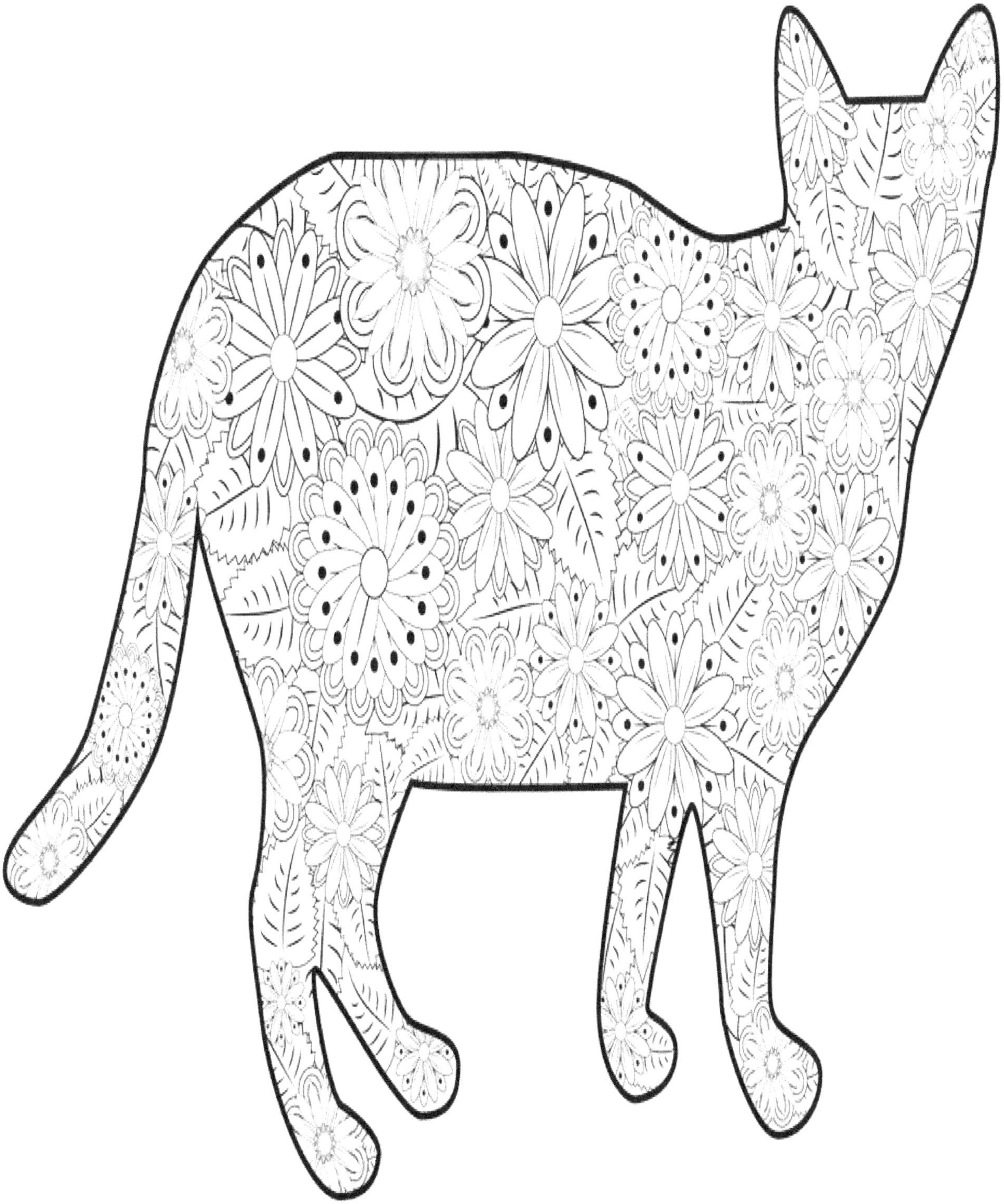

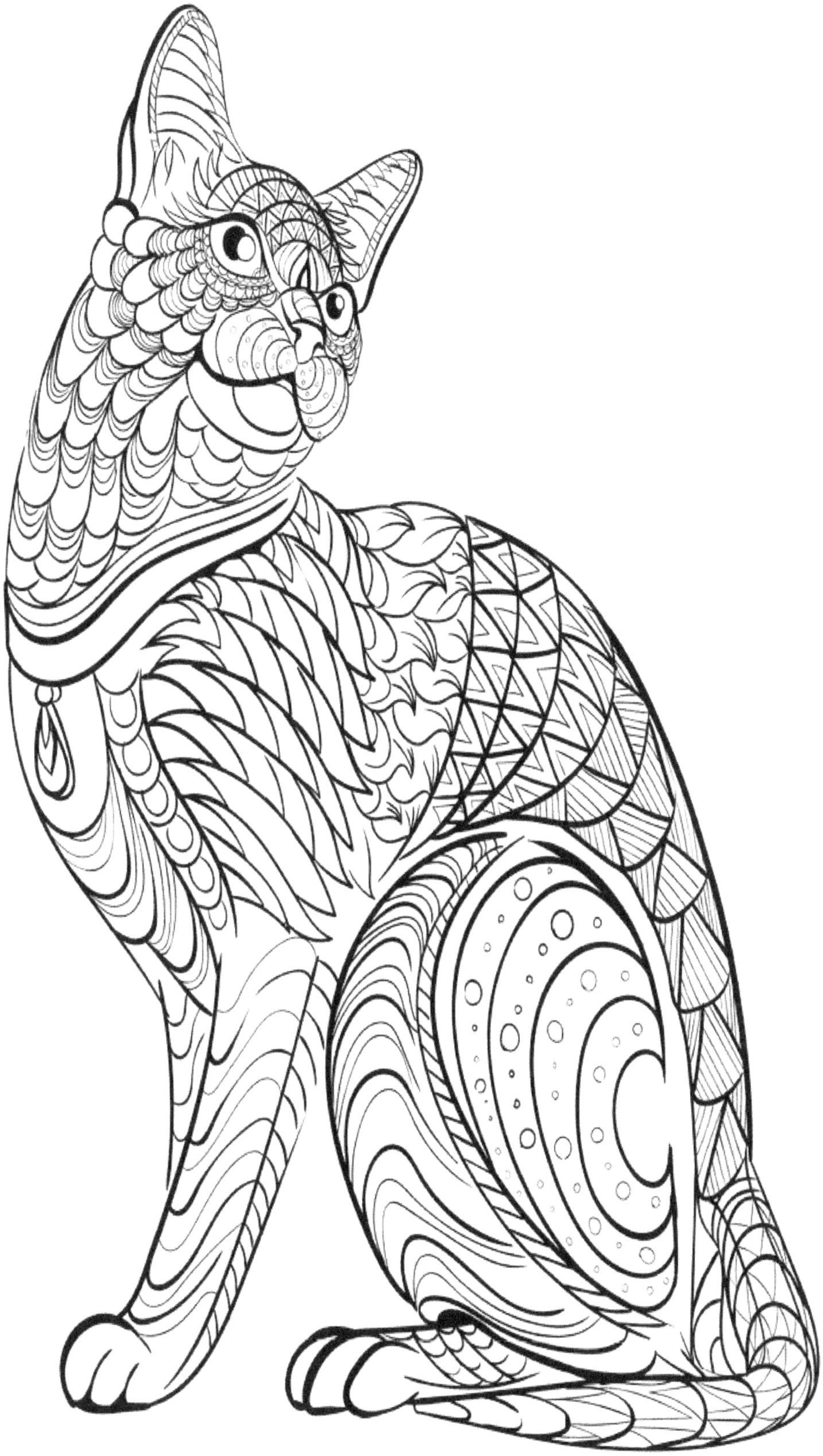

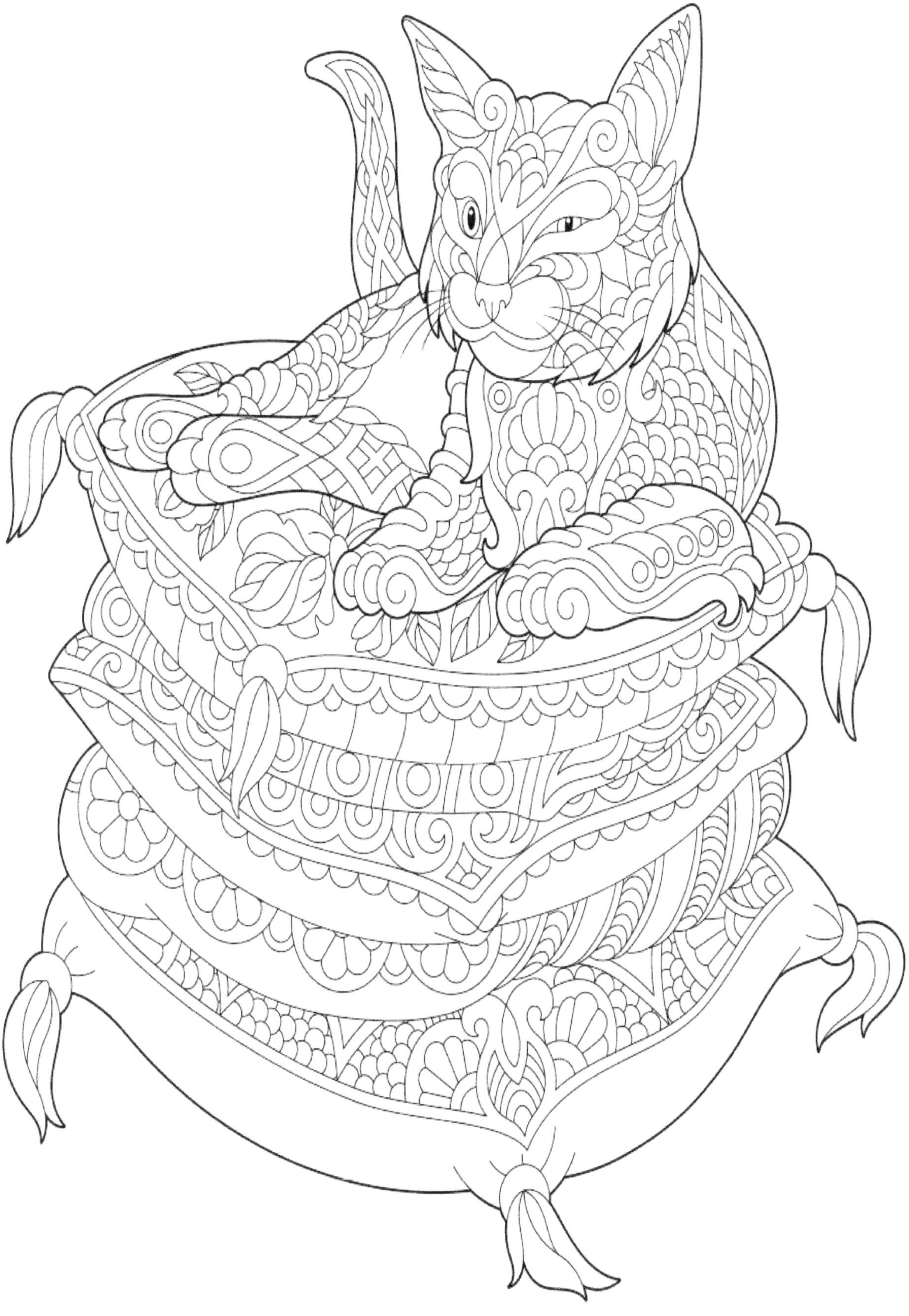

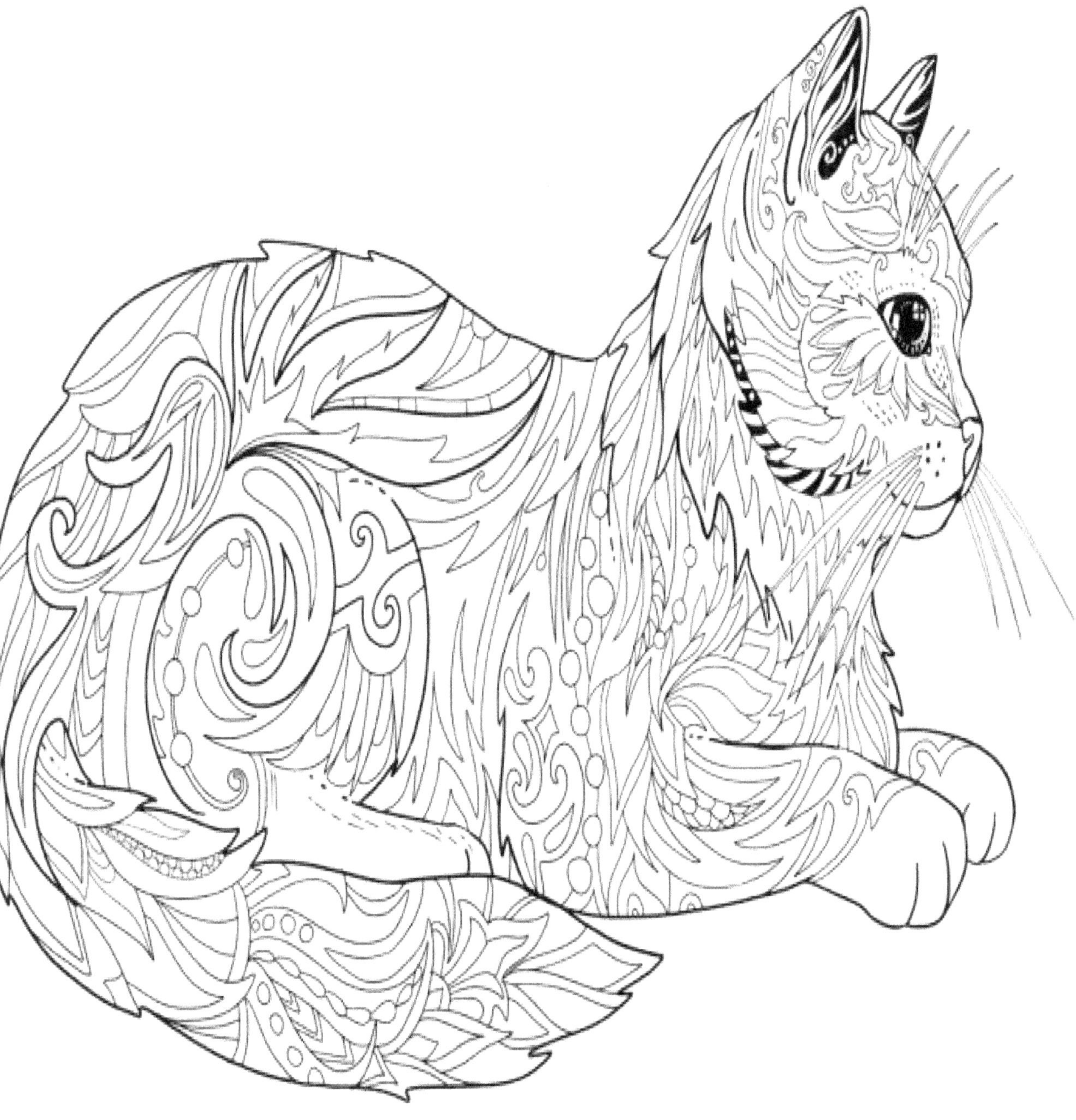

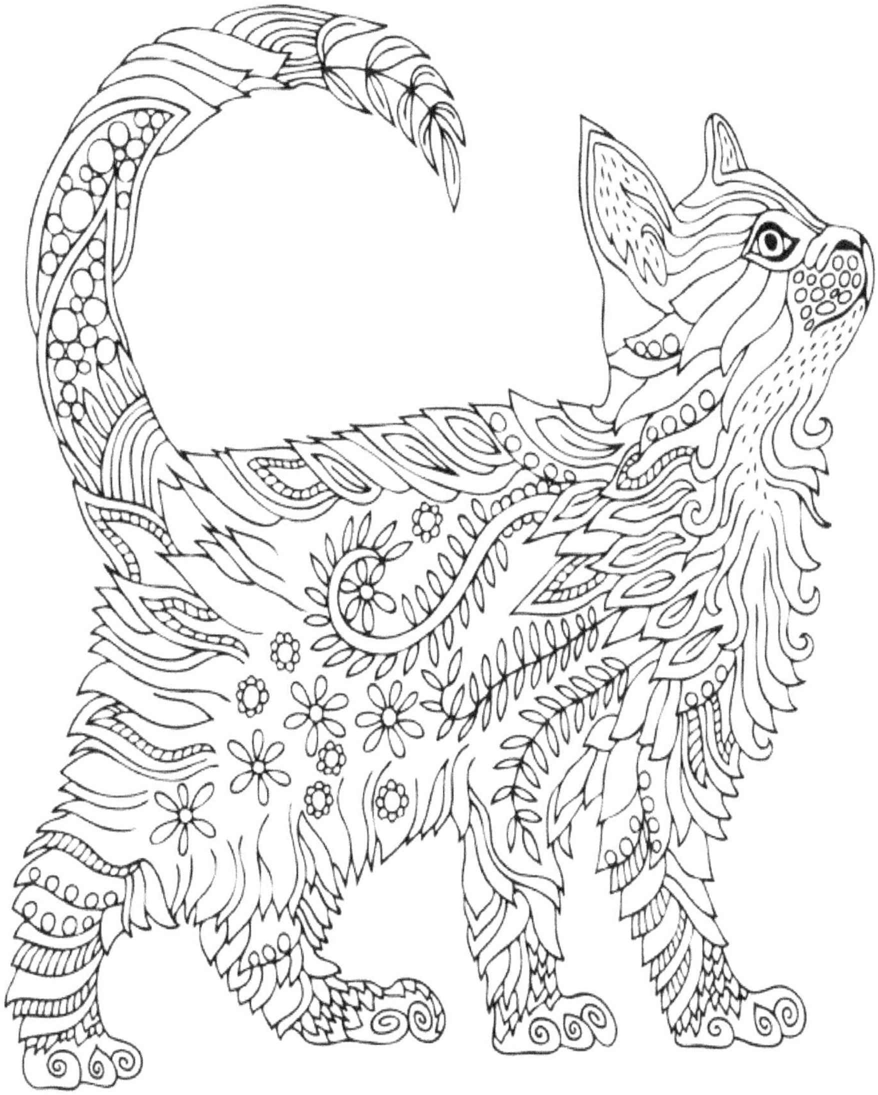

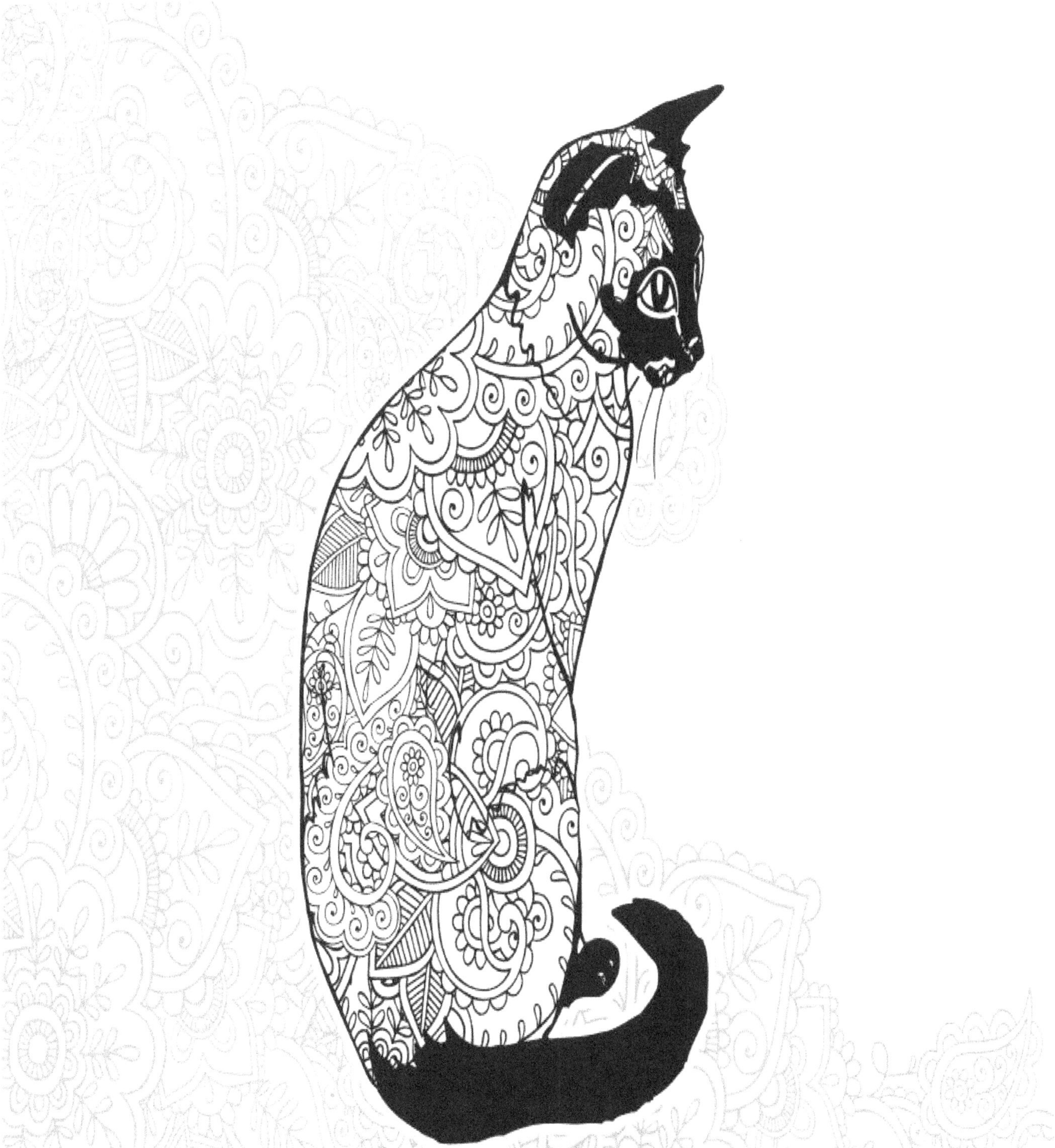

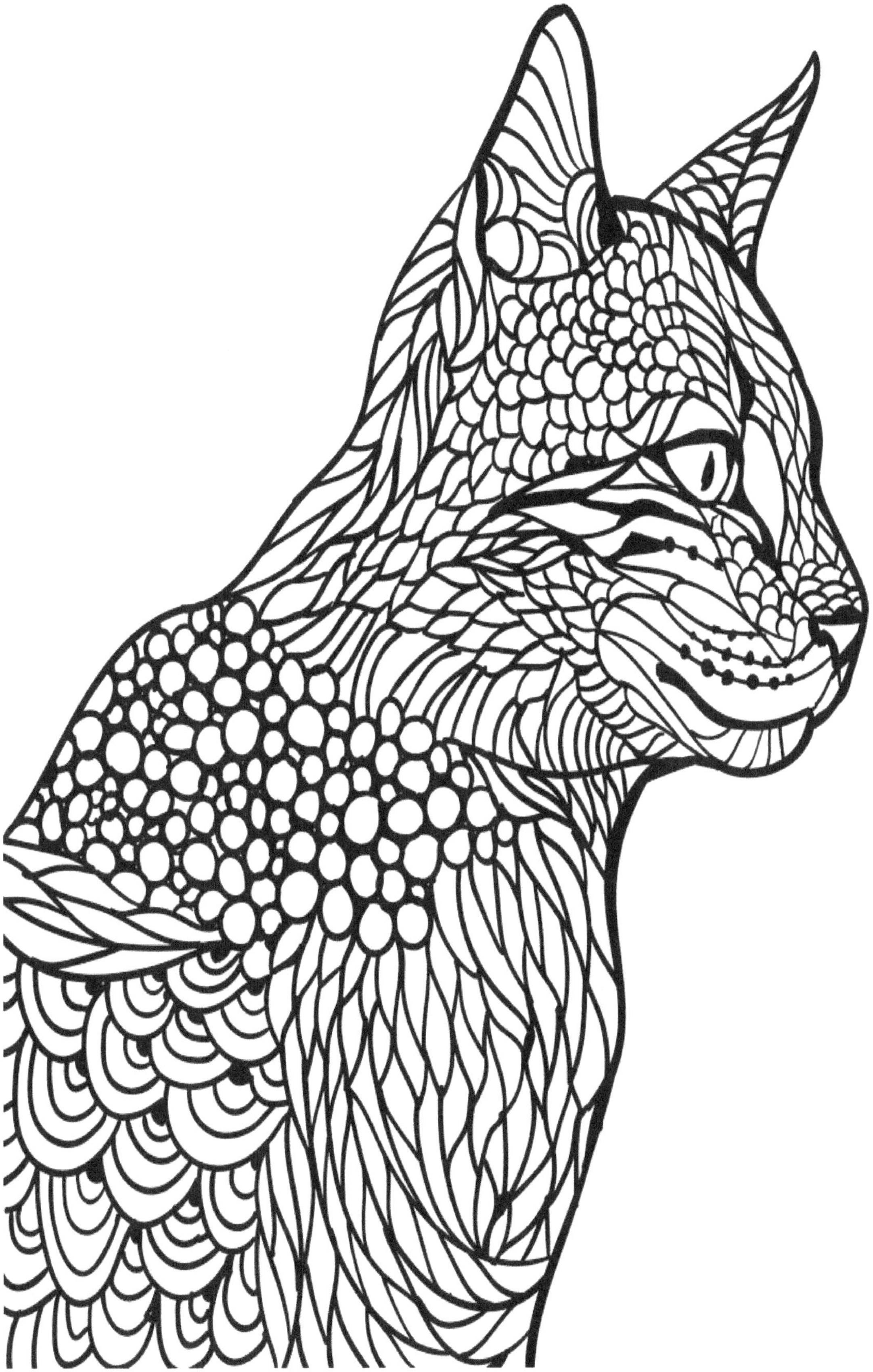

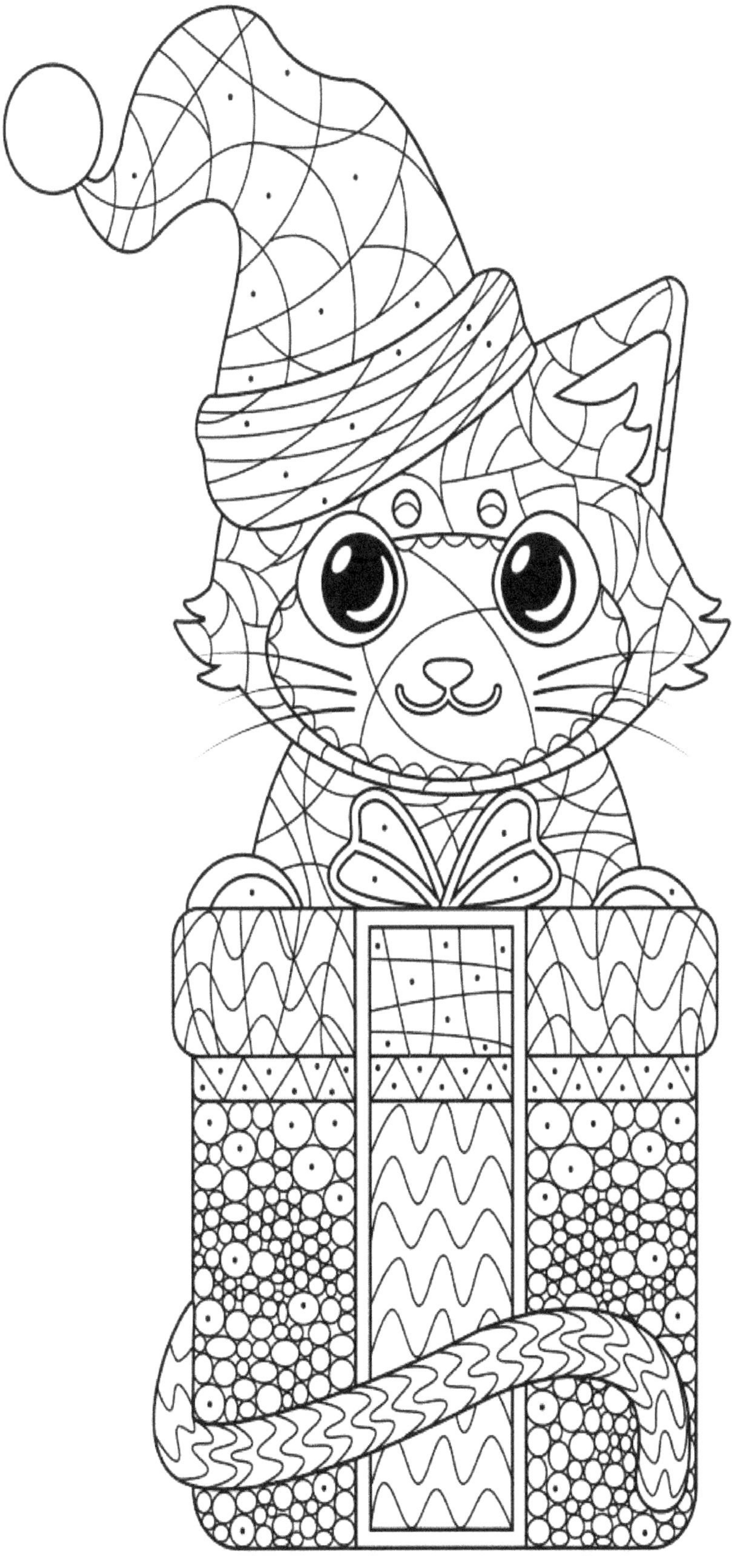

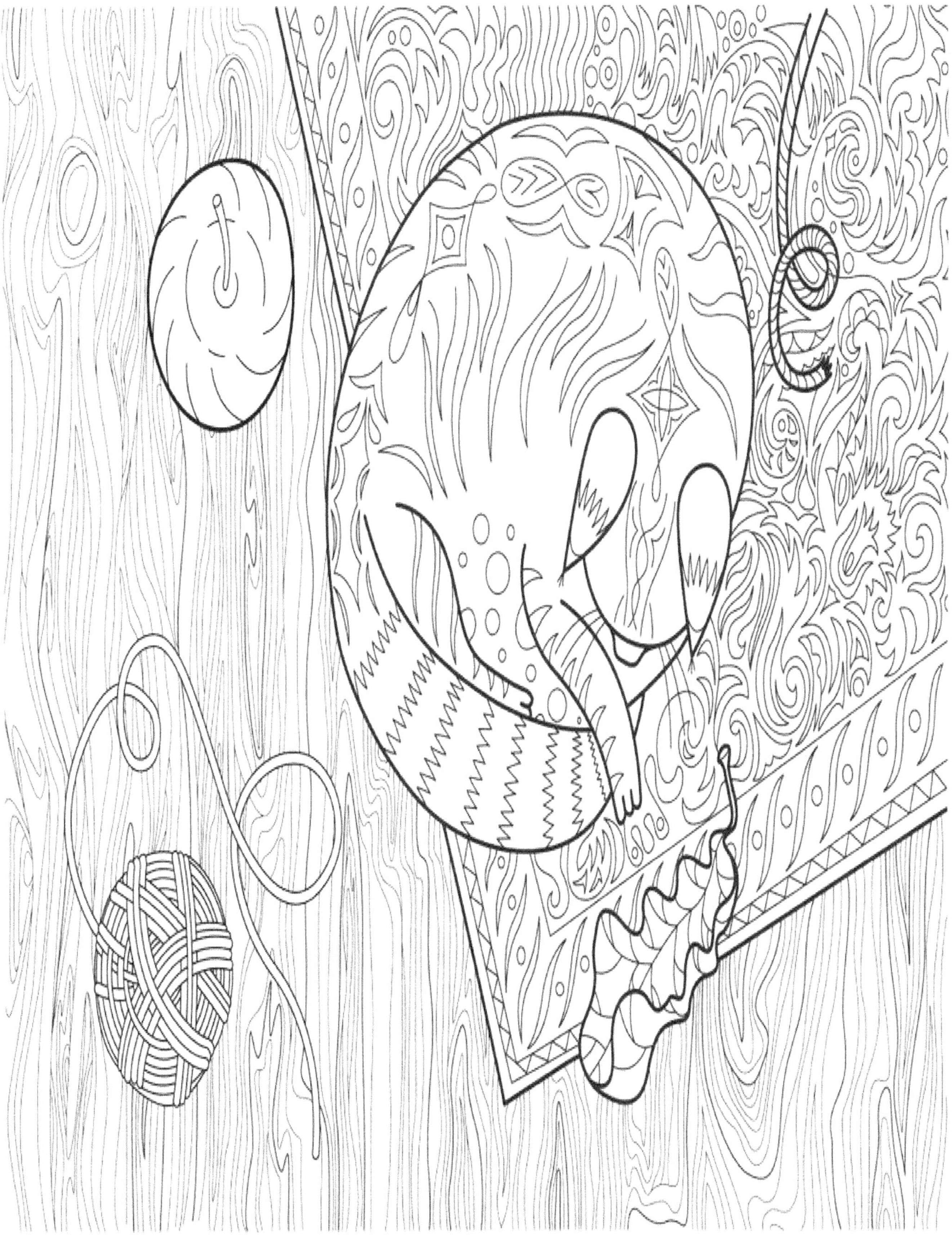

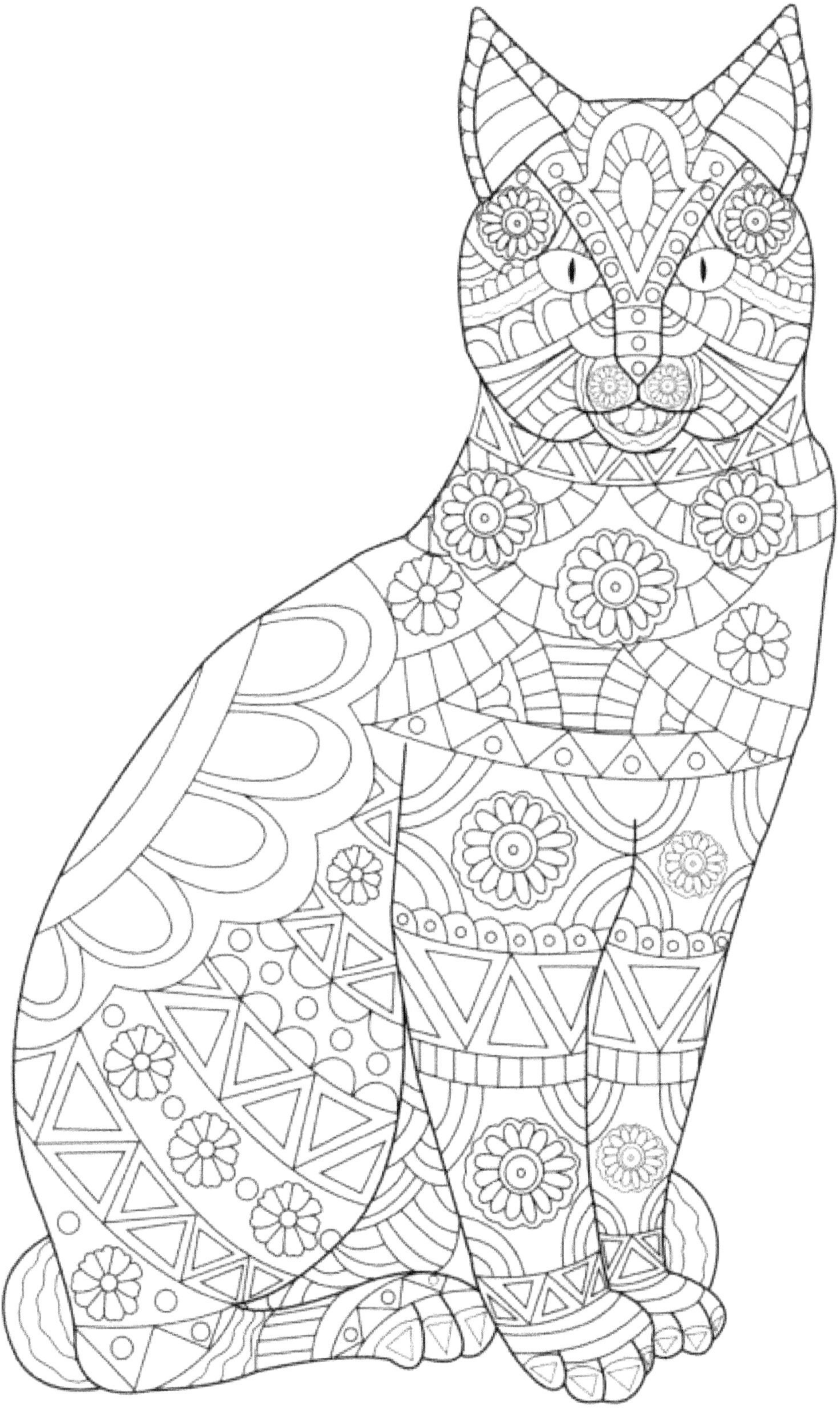

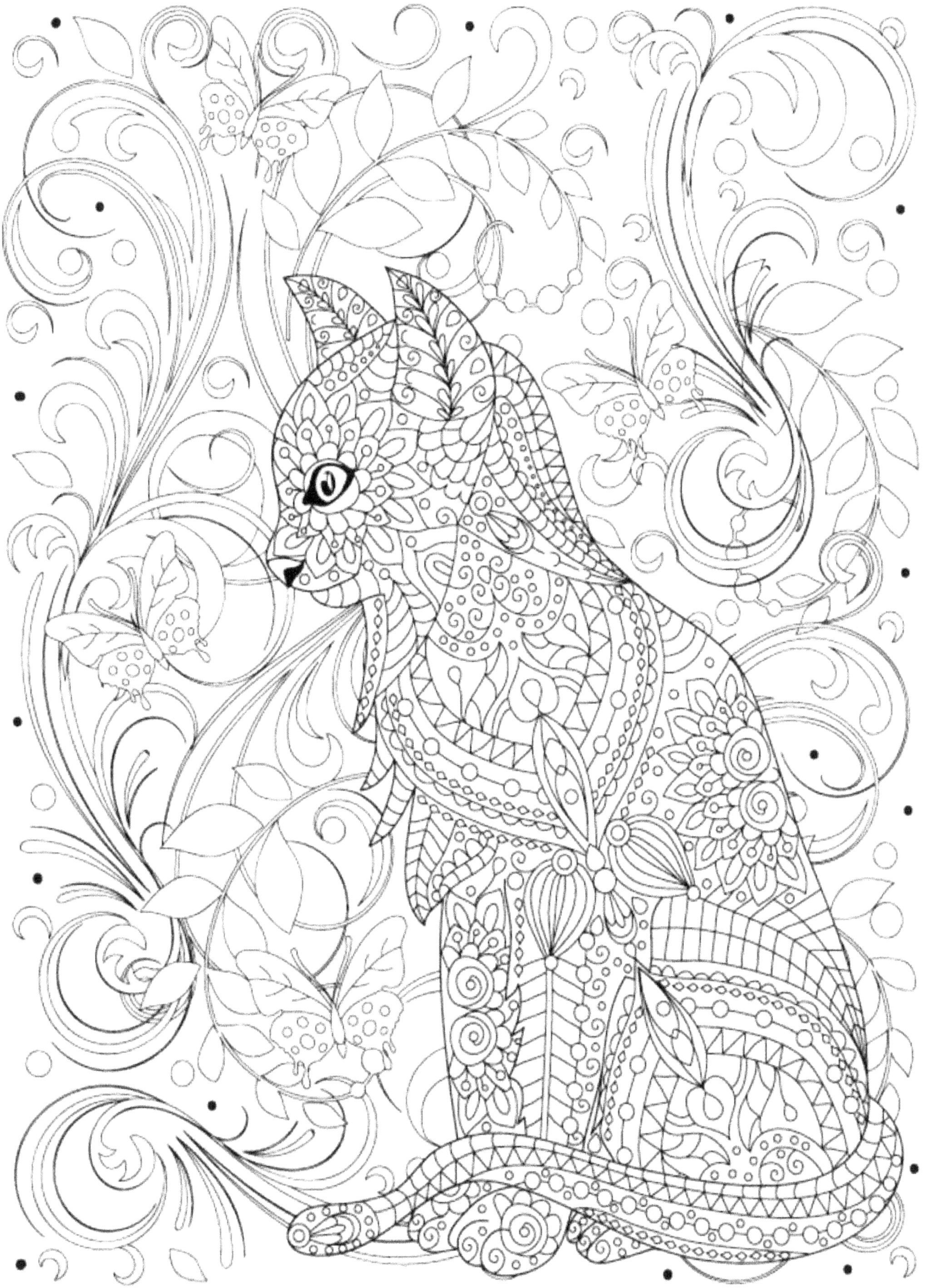

www.ingramcontent.com/pod-product-compliance
Lightning Source LLC
Chambersburg PA
CBHW081523220526
45467CB00010B/3028
* 9 7 9 8 6 9 2 2 9 6 5 0 4 *